About the Author

JAMES C. HUMES is a lawyer and public speaker who has served in the White House, the State Department, and the Pennsylvania state legislature. He has lectured in all fifty states and in twenty countries. He is a former Woodrow Wilson Fellow at the Smithsonian Institution's Woodrow Wilson International Center for Scholars.

The Wit & Wisdom of
FDR

Also by James C. Humes

Which President Killed a Man?

Speak Like Churchill, Stand Like Lincoln

Eisenhower and Churchill:
  The Partnership That Saved the World

Nixon's Ten Commandments of Statecraft

The Wit & Wisdom of Abraham Lincoln

The Wit & Wisdom of Benjamin Franklin

Confessions of a White House Ghost Writer

Citizen Shakespeare: A Social and Political Portrait

"My Fellow Americans":
  Presidential Addresses That Shaped History

The Wit & Wisdom of Winston Churchill

The Sir Winston Method

Talk Your Way to the Top

Podium Humor

More Podium Humor

Churchill: Speaker of the Century

How to Get Invited to the White House

Speaker's Treasury of Anecdotes about the Famous

Instant Eloquence

The Wit & Wisdom of

FDR

James C. Humes

HARPER PERENNIAL

NEW YORK • LONDON • TORONTO • SYDNEY • NEW DELHI • AUCKLAND

HARPER ● PERENNIAL

THE WIT & WISDOM OF FDR. Copyright © 2008 by James C. Humes. All rights reserved. Printed in the United States of America. No part of this book may be used or reproduced in any manner whatsoever without written permission except in the case of brief quotations embodied in critical articles and reviews. For information address HarperCollins Publishers, 10 East 53rd Street, New York, NY 10022.

HarperCollins books may be purchased for educational, business, or sales promotional use. For information please write: Special Markets Department, HarperCollins Publishers, 10 East 53rd Street, New York, NY 10022.

FIRST EDITION

Designed by Jamie Kerner-Scott

Library of Congress Cataloging-in-Publication Data is available upon request.

ISBN: 978-0-06-123148-3

08 09 10 11 12 OV/RRD 10 9 8 7 6 5 4 3 2 1

Acknowledgments

F IRST, I WANT TO thank my son-in-law, Cecil Quillen III, who
pressed me to write this book.

Then my wife, Dianne, who listened to my telling of the
FDR anecdotes for honing and tailoring.

Linda Graham, my typist, who had to decipher my handwriting and do many redrafts.

Finally, my agent, Carol Mann, and my editor, Hugh Van
Dusen.

Contents

Introduction   xi

FDR's Sayings   1

FDR's Saints and Sinners   31

FDR by His Friends and Foes   38

FDR's Firsts   47

FDR's Fables   63

FDR's Famous Phrases   150

FDR's Memorable Speeches   164

Milestones   200

Bibliography   202

Introduction

WHAT IS A REGISTERED Republican doing writing this affectionate work about FDR? In fact, I am more than a nominal Republican. I was a White House speechwriter for several Republican presidents.

But the first president I ever remember is Franklin Delano Roosevelt and the first presidential election that I recall was the Roosevelt-Willkie race in 1940. Indeed, the first tie I ever wore was a navy-blue one with the name Wendell Willkie printed in small letters many times sloping down from left to right.

My father was a judge and local Republican leader who was often mentioned as a gubernatorial prospect until he died at the age of forty-two in 1943. Both my parents were eastern internationalist Republicans who daily read the *New York Herald Tribune* and weekly perused Henry Luce's *Time* magazine.

Our city, Williamsport in upstate Pennsylvania, was Republican. On our block, there lived only one Democrat, an Episcopalian clergyman. My father, who served on the National Board of Foreign Missions of the Presbyterian Church (along with John Foster Dulles), argued both theology and politics with our neighbor across the street. As a judge, father particularly bridled at Roosevelt's attempted packing of the Supreme Court (Supreme Court Justice Owen Roberts of Philadelphia was a friend). He was also incensed by FDR's breaking George Washington's precedent to run for a third term. But the judge and clergyman maintained their good humor. The rector once pinned a Republican button on my mother's back that said, "We don't want Eleanor either," which was my mother's name, as well as that of the first lady.

My parents, unlike the Midwest Taft Republicans of the day, supported Roosevelt on the need for the draft and the delivery of war shipments to Britain. Churchill was a hero in our house. My first long trousers were an exact copy of an RAF uniform with wings, which my mother had won for her leadership in the "Bundles for Britain" World War II relief organization.

My mother took Willkie's defeat harder than my father. She was so sure that he would win that when he lost, she took to her bed for two days.

The first time I remember hearing President Roosevelt was his "Day of Infamy" speech, the day after the bombing of Pearl Harbor. My father and mother had all three of us boys listen to his talk on the Philco radio in the living room. The next day my father tried to enlist, but he was rejected because of his judicial office.

The following spring my Republican father wrote to a Harvard Law School classmate, who was a personal friend of the president, and asked him for a letter of introduction to FDR. In February of that year, a restored Williamsburg in Virginia had opened to the public. We soon combined a trip to Williamsburg at cherry blossom time with a visit to the nation's capital.

Our new sky-blue Lincoln Zephyr stopped at Pennsylvania Avenue in front of the White House, where my father, armed with a letter from his friend as an introduction, walked in without an appointment to see if he could meet President Roosevelt.

My mother did not approve of what she called "fraternizing with the enemy." She smoldered for two hours, as my two older brothers roughhoused and scrapped in the backseat. Then my father appeared, looking sheepishly toward my irate mother. "Eleanor, I knew I shouldn't have talked to him. The S.O.B. charmed me."

Two years later was another election year. The first convention I remember listening to was the Democratic Convention and the fight that dumped Vice President Henry Wallace for a man named Truman.

In that election year of 1944, my now-widowed mother wore her Dewey-Bricker badge for the last two weeks of the campaign. But in her comments to her sons, she was less than confident of a Republican victory.

Actually, the manager of the Dewey campaign told me years later that their internal polls just after Labor Day had them only four points behind. My son-in-law, Cecil Quillen, was hosting a dinner in 1997 for the ninety-two-year-old Herbert Brownell (attorney general under Eisenhower) at the Brook, a private New York club. The other special guest of honor was my daughter's St. Paul's School former classmate Thomas E. Dewey III. Young Dewey and Brownell had never met before. Brownell told us that their best issue in 1944 was Roosevelt's health, which could only be hinted at as "old and tired leadership."

That fall I remember one campaign leaflet a Republican ward leader dropped off at our door. It featured Communist Party President Earl Browder together with Roosevelt. I showed it to my mother, who dismissed it, saying, "I don't need such tripe to vote against Roosevelt."

My mother, though, was scathing in her comments on Roosevelt's early November open motorcar ride through New York City on a wet and chilly day.

"They put pancake makeup on that sick man's face and then propped him up for that campaign stunt." Less than half a year later, Roosevelt was dead. On our street, there were Republicans actually celebrating the death of "that man in the White House."

I walked into our house and said elatedly, "Roosevelt's dead, and the people up the street are having a beer party."

My mother replied, "James Calhoun Humes, I am deeply chagrined at your behavior, and if your father was alive, he might have spanked you!" "Chagrin" was her word that signaled maternal anger at egregious behavior, and that word, coupled with her former schoolteacher glare, never failed to trigger tears.

She continued, "Franklin Delano Roosevelt was our president. We may have disagreed with many of his policies, but we must pay our respect to the office and the man who holds it. Your father would have been ashamed of your unpatriotic act against America. He would have severely disciplined you."

In the six decades since, my respect for the office has grown and, along with it, my respect for the ordeal it takes to get to the White House and the pressures on those who hold that office.

I remember years later, during Watergate, being at a dinner party in New York City when Nixon was being harshly criticized by the mostly Republican members at the table.

Margaret Truman Daniel, President Truman's daughter, who was also at the dinner, was asked her comments. "Everyone knows my politics, but after living in the White House while my father was being attacked, I made up my mind to refrain from comments regarding a president while in office." (Truman, by the way, is the only president to receive a lower Gallup approval rating than Nixon. Truman received it in February 1952.)

To me, presidents were a part of our history, and I fell in love with American history. In my teens, I clipped and collected quotations and anecdotes about presidents. As part of the pre-TV radio and records generation, I played 78 records of the thirties and forties. My favorites were recordings of Churchill and Roosevelt, and I soon could mimic them and recite some of their speeches by heart.

I would meet Prime Minister Churchill in London in May 1953, when I was an English-Speaking Union scholar at a British school. When I said I wanted to enter government, Churchill said, "Young man, study history. In history lie all the secrets of statecraft."

Former President Truman echoed the same advice when I spoke to him in the Senate Dining Room. (It was May 1960, and Truman was with fellow Missourian Senator Stuart Symington, whom Truman was supporting for president against Kennedy). I told him, "Mr. President, I'm a Republican who greatly admires your foreign policy achievements, and I want to enter politics."

"Read American history," Truman replied, "and tell the truth. You Republicans think I was giving you hell, but I was only telling the truth, and you thought it was hell."

I never met Roosevelt. But I heard him on the radio and remember the Warner Pathe newsreels we watched at the movie theater after the previews and before the cartoons and the regular feature, and I think the "politically correct" have done a disservice in the Washington Memorial to this president who dominated the first half of the twentieth century.

Roosevelt is shown in a wheelchair. We never saw him in a wheelchair during the war in any photos or newsreels. The look on his face is a grimace suggesting a constipated sitter on the morning throne. It is a far cry from that jaunty look of high humor and optimism that lifted so many spirits. And nowhere to be seen was his cigarette in its holder, which was just as much a part of his image as Churchill's cigar. In the quotations engraved above the memorial, one looks in vain for his Pearl Harbor phrase—"a date which will live in infamy." A further note of absurdity is that above each quotation are the same words in Braille. But they are so high above the ground that even a basketball player like seven-foot Shaquille O'Neal couldn't reach them on tiptoes.

I had the pleasure of dining twice with two of Roosevelt's sons —the youngest, John, at a Saint Nicholas Society dinner in the eighties in New York (who incidentally seconded Nixon's nomination for the presidency in 1960) and the oldest son, James, at a lunch that opened the Nixon Presidential Library in 1990. Both men said that the one singular quality their father possessed was his unwavering good humor and high spirits, even during his ordeal with polio.

I would like to think both sons would approve of my affectionate portrayal of their father.

FDR's Sayings

I N *Bartlett's Familiar Quotations*, the premier collection of noted sayings, only one American has more citations under his name than Franklin Roosevelt. (No, it is not Lincoln but Mark Twain, who was Roosevelt's favorite author.)

That is not surprising when one considers that Roosevelt presided over two of the most climactic times in American history—the Great Depression and World War II.

But it is a tribute to the lilt, pith, and wit of so many of his utterances. Roosevelt employed the use of speechwriters. Some of them were very talented, such as Pulitzer Prize winners Robert Sherwood and Archibald MacLeish. Playwrights like Sherwood and MacLeish, as well as other wordsmiths, possess the skills to craft a memorable line through the use of repetition, rhyme, and alliteration, as well as the arresting metaphor. All of these can be noted in the following observations by FDR.

Bartlett's, which includes writers and poets, as well as generals and statesmen, from classical to contemporary times, has only limited space in a one-volume book. It weighs three factors in considering what to include—the familiarity of the saying, the fame of the one uttering it, and the length of the statement. Entire speeches—such as the Gettysburg Address—are a singular exception.

The following quotations fill in the details in this political portrait of the thirty-second president. The selections manifest his wisdom, wit, and robust personality.

Action
- This is no time for fear, for reaction, or for timidity.
- We shall strive for perfection. We shall not achieve it immediately—but we shall strive. We may make mistakes, but they must never be mistakes which result from faintness of heart or abandonment of moral principle.
- We oppose a mere period of coma in our national life.

Aggression
- Against naked force, the only possible defense is naked force. The aggressor makes the rules for such a war; the defenders

have no alternative but matching destruction with more destruction, slaughter with greater slaughter.

America

- Self-help and self-control are the essence of the American tradition.
- I sometimes think the saving grace of America lies in the fact that the overwhelming majority of Americans are possessed of two great qualities—a sense of humor and a sense of proportion.
- The Almighty God has blessed our land in many ways. He has given our people stout hearts and strong arms with which to strike mighty blows for freedom and truth. He has given to our country a faith which has become the hope of all peoples in an anguished world.

Appeasement

- We must always be wary of those who with sounding brass and the tinkling cymbal preach the "ism" of appeasement.
- We have never had the illusion that peace and freedom could be based on weakness.
- No nation can appease the Nazis. No man can tame a tiger

into a kitten by stroking it. There can be no appeasement with ruthlessness. There can be no reasoning with an incendiary bomb.

Art

- Art is not a treasure in the past or an importation from another land, but part of the present life of all the living and creating peoples.
- A world turned into a stereotype, a society converted into a regiment, a life translated into a routine, make it difficult for either art or artists to survive. Crush individuality in society, and you crush art as well. Nourish the conditions of a free life, and you nourish the arts, too.

Big Business

- Beware of that profound enemy of the free enterprise system who pays lip service to free competition—but also labels every antitrust prosecution as a "persecution."
- Private enterprise, indeed, became too private. It became privileged enterprise, not free enterprise.
- The struggle against private monopoly is a struggle for, and

not against, American business. It is a struggle to preserve individual enterprise and economic freedom.

- Private enterprise is ceasing to be free enterprise and is becoming a cluster of private collectivisms, masking itself as a system of free enterprise after the American model. It is, in fact, becoming a concealed cartel system after the European model.

Books

- Books cannot be killed by fire. People die, but books never die. No man and no force can abolish memory. . . . Books are weapons, and it is a part of your dedication always to make them weapons for man's freedom.

Campaign

- Never let your opponent pick the battleground on which to fight. If he picks one, stay out of it and let him fight all by himself.

Challenge

- I propose to sail ahead. I feel sure that your hopes and your help are with me. For to reach a port, we must sail—sail, not lie at anchor, sail not drift.

Civil Liberties

- It is a good thing to demand liberty for ourselves and for those who agree with us, but it is a better thing and rarer thing to give liberty to others who do not agree with us.

Compassion

- Human kindness has never weakened the stamina or softened the fiber of a free people. A nation does not have to be cruel to be tough.

Congress

- It is the duty of the president to propose, and it is the privilege of the Congress to dispose.

Conservation

- The nation that destroys its soil destroys itself.

Conservative

- The true conservative is the man who has a real concern for injustices and takes thought against the day of reckoning.
- A conservative is a man with two perfectly good legs who has never learned to walk forward.

JAMES C. HUMES

- A reactionary is a somnambulist walking backwards.

Constitution

- The Constitution of the United States was a layman's document, not a lawyer's contract. This great layman's document was a charter of general principles. . . .

    But for one hundred and fifty years, we have had an unending struggle between those who would preserve this original broad concept of the Constitution as a layman's instrument of government and those who would shrivel the Constitution into a lawyer's contract.

- It was with farsighted wisdom that the framers of the Constitution brought together in one magnificent phrase three great concepts—"common defense," "general welfare," and "domestic tranquility."

    More than a century and a half later, we still believe with them that our best defense is the promotion of our general welfare and domestic tranquility.

- Our constitution of 1787 was not a perfect document; it is not perfect yet, but it provided a firm base upon which all manner of men of all races, colors, and creeds could build our solid structure of democracy.

Consumer

- I believe that we are on the threshold of a fundamental change in our popular economic thought, that in the future we are going to think less about the producer and more about the consumer.

Crisis

- Nationwide thinking, nationwide planning, and nationwide action are the three great essentials to prevent nationwide crises for future generations to struggle through.
- Out of every crisis, every tribulation, every disaster, mankind rises with some share of greater knowledge, of higher decency, of purer purpose.

Debt

- You cannot borrow your way out of debt, but you can invest your way into a sounder future.
- Our national debt, after all, is an internal debt, owed not only *by* the nation but *to* the nation. If our children have to pay the interest, they will pay that interest to *themselves*.

Defense

- Our security is not a matter of weapons alone. The arm that wields them must be strong, the eye that guides them clear, the will that directs them indomitable.
- The core of our defense is the faith we have in the institution we defend.

Deficit Spending

- Too often governments have floundered on the rocks of fiscal instability. I pledge to you a balanced budget [1932].

Democracy

- What the American people demanded in 1933 was not less democracy but more democracy—and this is what they got.
- Democracy is not a static thing. It is an everlasting march.
- Democracy is the practice of self-government and is a covenant among free men to respect the rights and liberties of their fellow man.
- Under democratic government, the poorest are no longer necessarily the most ignorant part of society. I agree with the saying of one of our famous statesmen [Jefferson], who devoted himself to the principle of majority rule. "I respect the aristoc-

racy of learning; I deplore the plutocracy of wealth; but thank God for the democracy of the heart."

- Democracy is not just a word to be shouted at political rallies and then put back into the dictionary after election day. The service of democracy must be something more than mere lip service.
- Democracy is the one form of society which guarantees to every new generation of men the right to imagine and to attempt to bring to pass a better world.

Democratic Party

- Our party must be a party of liberal thought, of planned action, of enlightened international outlook, and of the greatest good to the greatest number of our citizens.

Depression

- Some economists are trying to figure out what it was that hit us back in 1929. I am not a professional economist, but I think I know. What hit us was a decade of debauchery, of group selfishness—the sole objective expressed in the thought "every man for himself, and let the devil take the hindmost." And the result was that about 98 percent of the American population turned out to be "the hindmost."

Dictatorship

- The United States will never survive as a happy and fertile oasis of liberty surrounded by a cruel desert of dictatorship.
- No dictator in history has ever dared to run the gauntlet of a really free election.

Diplomacy

- More than an end to war, we want an end to the beginning of all wars—an end to this brutal, inhuman, and thoroughly impractical method of settling the differences between governments.

Diversity

- We are a nation of many nationalities, many races, many religions—bound together by a single unity, the unity of freedom and equality.

  Whoever seeks to set one nationality against another seeks to degrade all nationalities.

  Whoever seeks to set one race against another seeks to enslave all races.

  Whoever seeks to set one religion against another seeks to destroy all religion.

- No democracy can long survive which does not accept as fundamental to its very existence the recognition of the rights of minorities.

Economy

- Overproduction, underproduction, and speculation are three evil sisters who distill the troubles of unsound inflation and disastrous deflation.

Education

- The greatest single resource of this country is its youth, and no progressive government cannot afford [to meet] the needs of its future citizens for adequate schooling and for that useful work which establishes them as part of the economy.
- Freedom to learn is the first necessity of guaranteeing that man himself shall be self-reliant enough to be free.
- Knowledge—that is education in the true sense—is our best protection against unreasoning prejudice and panic-making fear, whether engendered by special interest, illiberal minorities, or panic-stricken leaders.

Environment

- Government cannot close its eyes to the pollution of waters, to the erosion of soil, to the slashing of forests any more than it can close its eyes to the need for slum clearance and schools and bridges.
- We have been fighting Nature. Now it is time for us to cooperate with Nature.
- We believe that the material resources of America should serve the human resources of America.

Equality

- Inside the polling booth, every American man and woman stands as the equal of every other American man and woman. There they have no superiors. There they have no masters, save their own minds and consciences.

Fascism

- In this world of ours, in other lands, there are some people who in times past have lived and fought for freedom and seem to have grown weary to carry on their fight. They have sold their heritage for the illusion of democracy. They have yielded up their democracy.

Fear

- The only thing we have to fear is fear itself—nameless, un-reasoning, unjustified terror which paralyzes needed effort to convert retreat into advance.

Freedom

- True individual freedom cannot exist without economic security and independence. People who are hungry and out of a job are the stuff of which dictatorships are made. In the truest sense, freedom cannot be bestowed; it must be achieved.
- We too, born to freedom and believing in freedom, are willing to maintain freedom. We and all others who believe as deeply as we do would rather die on our feet than live on our knees.
- But we have learned that freedom, in itself, is not enough. Freedom of speech is of no use to a man who has nothing to say. Freedom of worship is of no use to a man who has lost his God.

Free Enterprise

- I am the best friend the profit system ever had.

Future

- The future is full of possibilities of adventure, no matter what its dangers—the only thing we must *not* lose is our capacity to meet what comes with a free spirit and an open mindw.

"Good Neighbor Policy"

- It is time that every citizen in every one of the American republics recognizes that the Good Neighbor Policy means that harm to one republic means harm to every republic. We have all recognized the principle of independence. It is time we recognize the *privilege* of interdependence—one upon another.
- [The policy of the Good Neighbor] is a policy which can never be unilateral. In stressing it, the American republics appreciate, I am confident, that it is a bilateral, a multilateral policy and fair-dealing, which implies it must be reciprocated.
- In the field of world policy, I would dedicate this nation to the policy of the good neighbor.

Government

- It is the purpose of the government to see that not only the legitimate interests of the few are protected but that the welfare and the rights of the many are conserved.

Immigrants

- The overwhelming majority of those who came from the nations of the Old World to our American shores were not the laggards, not the timorous, not the failures.

    They came to us speaking many tongues, but a single language, the universal language of human aspiration.

Inequality

- We find our population suffering from old inequalities, little changed by sporadic remedies. In spite of our efforts and in spite of all talk, we have not weeded out the overprivileged and we have not effectively lifted up the underprivileged.

International Relations

- Today we are faced with the preeminent fact that if civilization is to survive the science of human relationship—it must demand the ability of all peoples, of all kinds, to live together in the same world in peace.

Isolationism

- Those Americans who believe that we could live under the

illusion of isolationism wanted the American eagle to imitate the tactics of the ostrich. Now many of those same people, afraid that we may be sticking our necks out, want our national bird to be turned into a turtle. But we prefer to retain the eagle as it is—flying high and striking hard.

- War may be "declared"; peace cannot. It must be established by mutual consent. We cannot anchor this ship of state in this world tempest, nor can we return to the placid harbor of long years ago.
- We are not isolationists, except insofar as we seek to isolate ourselves completely from war. Yet we must remember that as long as war exists on earth, there will be some danger that even the nation which most ardently desires peace may be drawn into war.

Labor Day

- Labor Day symbolizes our determination to achieve an economic freedom for the average man which will give his political freedom reality.

Liberalism

- A liberal is a man who uses his legs and hands at the behest and command of his head.

- Liberalism becomes the protection of the farsighted conservative.

- Too many of those who prate about saving democracy are really only interested in saving things as they are. Democracy should concern itself also with things as they ought to be.

- We Americans everywhere must and shall choose the path of social justice—the only path that will lead to a permanent bettering of our lives is the path that our children must tread and their children must tread, the path of faith, the path of hope, and the path of love toward our fellow man.

- We are starting on something absolutely new, something in which we have very little experience to fall back on, something that has to be developed through what I call evolution. When people talk to you about the word "revolution" in this country, you tell them that they have one letter too many in the word.

- The vigor of our history comes largely from the fact that as a comparatively young nation we have gone fearlessly ahead doing things that were never done before.

James C. Humes

- America needs a government of constant progress along liberal lines. America requires that this progress be sane and that this progress be honest. America calls for a government with a soul.
- Years ago, President Wilson told me a story. He said that the greatest problem that the head of a progressive democracy had to face was not the criticism of reactionaries . . . but to reconcile and unite the progressive liberals themselves.

Liberty
- Our government is based on the belief that a people can be strong and free, that civilized men need no restraint but that imposed by themselves against abuse of freedom.

Materialism
- Physical strength can never permanently withstand the impact of spiritual force.

Memorials
- We in America do not build monuments to war. We do not build monuments to conquest. We build monuments to commemorate the spirit of sacrifice in war—reminders of our desire for peace.

Militarism

- You cannot organize civilization around the core of militarism and at the same time expect reason to control human destinies.

Mind

- Men are not prisoners of fate, but only prisoners of their own minds.

Nation

- The driving force of a nation lies in its spiritual purpose made effective by free, tolerant, but unremitting national will.

Navy

- My heart shall always be with the navy.

Neutrality

- This nation will remain a neutral nation, but I cannot ask that every American remain neutral in thought as well. Every neutral nation has a right to take account of facts.

Parents

- The parents of our children are the guardians of our future citizens. They cannot evade the responsibility which is theirs through example and intelligent understanding to inspire and lay the groundwork for that type of character which does right under any circumstance and is able to withstand temptation.

Party Platform

- A party platform is a promissory note to the American electorate that is never paid.

Peace

- Peace, like war, can only succeed where there is a will to enforce it, and where there is available power to enforce it.
- Peace can endure only so long as humanity really insists upon it and is willing to work for it—and sacrifice for it.
- Peace, like charity, begins at home.

Politicians

- The future lies with those wise political leaders who realize that the great public is interested more in government than politics.

Presidency

- I never forget that I live in a house owned by all the American people and that I have been given their trust. . . . I want to be sure that neither battles nor burdens of office shall ever blind me to an intimate knowledge of the way the American people want to live and the simple purposes they put me here for.

Press

- By a free press I mean a press which is untrammeled by prejudice and unfettered by bias, which will serve no cause but that of truth and which recognizes no master but justice.

Principle

- The fate of America cannot depend on any one man. The greatness of America is grounded in principles and not on any single personality.

Propaganda

- Repetition does not transform a lie into a truth.

Public Health

- Public health is more than a local responsibility. Disease knows nothing about town lines, nor do bacilli undertake to inquire about local jurisdiction.

Public Office

- In our democracy, officers of the government are the servants and never the masters of the people.

Public Opinion

- A government can be no better than the public opinion that sustains them.

Purpose

- There is a mysterious circle in human events. To some generations, much is given. Of other generations, much is expected. This generation of Americans has a rendezvous with destiny.

Radicals

- A radical is a man with both feet firmly planted—in the air.
- You sometimes find something good in the radical fringe. In fact, we have got, as part of our social and economic govern-

ment, a whole lot of things which in my boyhood were considered lunatic fringe and yet they are now part of our economic life.

Reform

- A real economic cure must go to the killing of bacteria in the system rather than the treatment of external symptoms.

Regulation

- We have all suffered in the past from individualism run wild.

Religion

- Any candidate who brings any question of religion into politics in a manner wholly un-American and un-Christian is not fit to be the holder of any office.

Roosevelt (Himself)

- I am like a cat. I make a quick strike, then I relax.
- I am a juggler. I never let my right hand know what my left hand does.
- I call myself a little left of center.
- I may be totally inconsistent, and furthermore, I am willing to

mislead and tell untruths, if it will help to win the war.

- [To Orson Welles] You and I are the two best actors in America.
- [When asked about his politics] I am a Christian and a Democrat—that's all.

Sanctuary

- When a man has been away a long time, it is sometimes necessary for him to get to a place where he can see the forest as well as the trees.

Social Security

- We should forever banish the black shadow of old-age want.
- Poverty in old age should not be regarded either as a disgrace or necessarily as a result of a lack of thrift or energy. Usually, it is a mere by-product of modern industrial life.

Special Interests

- We oppose money in politics, we oppose the private control of national finances, we oppose the treatment of human beings as commodities, we oppose starvation wages, we oppose rule by groups or cliques.

Spending

- Too often, in recent history, liberal governments have been wrecked on rocks of loose fiscal policy [1932].
- Investment for prosperity can be made in a democracy.

Truth

- The truth is found when men are free to pursue it.

Unemployment

- Idle factories and idle workers profit no man.

Unions

- It is one of the characteristics of a free and democratic modern nation that it has free and independent labor unions.

Values

- The supreme values are spiritual. The hope of the world is that character which is built from the solid rock withstands triumphantly the storms of life.

Voting

- We can assert the most glorious, the most encouraging fact in all the world today—the fact that democracy is alive and going strong. We are telling the world that we are free—and we intend to remain free.

We are free to live and love and laugh. We face the world with courage and confidence.

We are Americans.

- Nobody will ever deprive the American people of the right to vote except the American people themselves—and the only way they can do that is by not voting.
- Let us never forget the government is *ourselves* and not an alien power over us. The ultimate rulers of our democracy are not the president and senators and government officials but the voters of this country.

War

- I have seen children starving. I have seen the agony of mothers and wives. I hate war.
- The motto of war is: let the strong survive; let the weak die. The motto of peace is: let the strong help the weak to survive.
- War is a contagion. It would be unworthy of a great nation to become inflamed by some one act of violence.

Wealth

- True wealth is not a static thing. It is a living thing made out of the disposition of men to create and distribute the good things of life with rising standards of living.
- It is an unfortunate human failing that a full pocketbook often groans more loudly than an empty stomach.

Welfare

- One of the duties of the state is that of caring for those of its citizens who find themselves victims of such perverse circumstances as make them unable to obtain even the necessities for mere existence without the aid of others. To those unfortunate citizens, aid must be extended by government—not as a matter of charity but as a matter of *social* duty.
- I am constantly thinking of all our people—unemployed and employed alike—of their human problems of food and clothing and homes and education and health and old age.
- I see one-third of a nation ill-housed, ill-clad, and ill-nourished.
- The test of our progress is not whether we add to the abundance of those who have too much; it is whether we provide enough for those who have too little.

JAMES C. HUMES

- By security, I do not mean just a living, just having enough to eat and a place to sleep. I mean living according to the American standard, a standard which provides a decent diet, a decent education, and a reasonable amount of leisure and recreation.

- Who would have thought a generation ago that people who lost their jobs would, for an appreciable period, receive unemployment insurance—that the needy, the blind, and the crippled children would receive some measure of protection which will reach down to the millions of Bob Cratchits, the Marthas, and the Tiny Tims of our own "four-room homes"?

- From the cradle to the grave—there ought to be social insurance.

- The people of America are in agreement in defending their liberties at any cost, and the first line of the defense lies in the protecting of economic security.

- A nation, like a person, has a body—a body that must be fed and clothed and housed, invigorated, and rested in a manner that measures up to the objectives of our time.

World

- We have learned to be citizens of the world; members of the human community.

World War II

- The militarists in Berlin and Tokyo started this war, but the massed, angered forces of humanity will end it.

Youth

- The temper of our youth has become more restless, more critical, more challenging. Flaming youth has become a flaming question, and youth wants to know what we propose to do about a society that hurts so many of them.
- We cannot build the future for youth, but we can build our youth for the future.

FDR's Saints and Sinners

F DR ONCE WROTE TO Winston Churchill, "It is fun to be in the same decade with you." In the generation that came to maturity in those years that included two World Wars, Roosevelt had observed some of the great political personalities of the time—Churchill up close and Hitler from afar.

Some of FDR's foes he liked and respected, such as Wendell Willkie. Some of his political allies, such as Joe Kennedy, he despised.

The political leader he most venerated was Theodore Roosevelt, his distant cousin and the uncle of his wife. The personality of Teddy Roosevelt captured the love of the people as no previous president had. Franklin Roosevelt, first as assistant secretary of the navy and then later as New York's governor, emulated Teddy. His New Deal echoed T. R.'s Square Deal.

Woodrow Wilson, in whose administration FDR served as

assistant secretary of the navy, inspired FDR's admiration but not his affection. Wilson's romantic idealism of a "war that would end all wars" and a "covenant" (the League of Nations) that would prevent future wars engaged FDR's enthusiasm and passion. This lofty internationalism of Wilson would shape FDR's later foreign policy.

Winston Churchill, British prime minister

- He is a tremendously vital person and in many ways an English version of Mayor [Fiorello] La Guardia [said after seeing Churchill in 1941].
- In this historic crisis, Britain is blessed with a brilliant and a great leader.
- It is fun to be in the same decade with you.
- I like Churchill. He's lovable and emotional and very human, but I don't want him to write the peace or carry it out.

Georges Clemenceau, World War I premier of France

- I knew at once I was meeting the greatest civilian in France [in 1917]. . . . . He is only seventy-seven years old, and people say he is getting younger every day.

Calvin Coolidge, U.S. President

- Calvin Coolidge would like to have God on his side, but he must have Andrew Mellon [Coolidge's secretary of the treasury and one of the richest men in America].
- Coolidge is as inarticulate to the extent of being thought a mystery. To stick a knife into ghosts is always hard.

Josephus Daniels, secretary of the navy under Woodrow Wilson

- You have taught me wisely and kept my feet on the ground when I was about to skyrocket.
- He's the funniest-looking hillbilly I have ever seen.

Charles de Gaulle, French general

- One day he wants to be Joan of Arc and the next day he wants to be a more worldly figure like [Georges] Clemenceau [French premier in World War I].

George V, British king

- The king has a nice smile and a very open, quiet, and cordial way of greeting one. . . . He is a delightful and easy person to talk to. [Comments on the British sovereign (the father of George VI) when Roosevelt met him at Buckingham Palace in 1917.]

Warren G. Harding, U.S. president

- Poor old Harding was perfectly honest himself but was not the kind of man who could ever tell the difference between a real friend and a crooked one, and he allowed himself to be surrounded by a pretty rotten crowd.

Adolf Hitler, Nazi dictator

- A wild man afflicted with paranoia and a Joan of Arc complex.

Harry Hopkins, FDR's chief political aide

- Harry is the perfect ambassador for my purposes. He doesn't know the meaning of the word "protocol." When he sees a piece of red tape, he just pulls out those old garden shears of his and clips it.

Louis J. Howe, FDR's first political adviser

- As a bookkeeper, Louis always added the amounts of checks he wrote instead of subtracting them.

Thomas Jefferson, U.S. president

- Thomas Jefferson faced the fact that men who will not fight for liberty can lose it.

- Thomas Jefferson believed—as we believe—in man. He believed, as we believe, that men are capable of determining their own government and that no king, no tyrant, no dictator can govern for them as wisely as they can govern for themselves.

Joseph Kennedy, business mogul and father of President John F. Kennedy

- This young man needs to have his wrists slapped rather hard [in 1918].
- To him, the future of capitalism is safer under a Hitler than under a Churchill.

Ernest J. King, U.S. admiral

- He shaves with a blowtorch and cuts his toenails with a torpedo net-cutter.

Arthur Krock, *New York Times* columnist

- He is that Tory Krockpot.

Marguerite ("Missy") LeHand, presidential secretary

- Missy is my conscience.

Huey Long, Louisiana governor and later senator

- That man is an influence for evil in the entire structure of our country.

Joe Martin, Republican minority leader

- He is one of that great historic trio which has consistently voted against the relief of agriculture—[Joe] Martin, [Bruce] Barton, and [Hamilton] Fish.

Theodore Roosevelt, FDR's cousin and U.S. president

- The greatest man I ever knew.
- Theodore Roosevelt, for me, rose up and battled against this squandering of our patrimony. He, for the first time, made the people as a whole conscious that the vast national domain and the natural resources of the country were the property of the nation itself and not the property of any class, regardless of its privileged status.
- In my first vote for president in 1904, I voted for the Republican Theodore Roosevelt, who was a better Democrat than the Democratic candidate.

36

Haile Selassie, emperor of Ethiopia

- I don't believe for a moment that Selassie is a scoundrel. (Perhaps I am prejudicial, for he keeps my photograph on his desk.) He is six centuries behind us—but he is a Christian.

Wendell Willkie, Republican presidential candidate

- He was a godsend to the country when we needed him the most.

Woodrow Wilson, U.S. president

- Let us feel that in everything we do still lives with us, if not the body, the great, indomitable, unquenchable, progressive soul of our Commander in Chief Woodrow Wilson.
- Of Woodrow Wilson, this can be said, that in time, when world councils were dominated by material considerations of greed and gain and revenge, he beheld the splendid vision. . . . He will be held in everlasting remembrance as a statesman who, when other men sought revenge and material gain, strove to bring nearer the day which should see the emancipation of conscience from power, and the substitution of freedom from force in the government of the world.

FDR by His Friends and Foes

GROVER CLEVELAND, THE PRESIDENT whom Franklin Roosevelt met as a little boy when he was taken to the White House, was once lauded in a Democratic National Convention nominating speech: "We love him for the enemies he has made."

Some readers might identify with those feelings when they note some of the vituperation uttered by some of FDR's foes.

A *New Yorker* cartoon showed some well heeled couples saying, "We're going to the movies to boo Roosevelt." "That man in the White House" was shortened to "that man" and, when expressed by a Republican, needed no more clarification. Nixon, Clinton, and now George W. Bush have attracted a legion of haters, but the venom hardly exceeded that shown towards FDR. A cartoon, which Roosevelt hung up in the White House, showed a little boy being reprimanded. "Johnny has just written a dirty word on the sidewalk." The word was "Roosevelt."

Yet for Democrats and those on the left, FDR was a champion—a knight in shining armor with his lance against the entrenched interest. There have been other progressive heroes, including his cousin, Theodore Roosevelt, but in his charm and sunny good humor, FDR inspired a legion of admirers that far exceeded TR's.

- His essence was force . . . the relish of power and command.
- His manner was so condescending. He'd talk to you as if you had been his longtime chauffeur or butler.

> DEAN ACHESON, treasury official and later secretary of
> state under President Truman

- [Roosevelt] is one of those aristocratic reformers. Their minds see large and generous horizons and above all reveal a unique intellectual gaiety of a kind that aristocratic education tends to produce. At the same time, they are on the side of everything that is new, progressive, rebellious, and untried.

> SIR ISAIAH BERLIN, political philosopher

- There was in the man a kind of narcissism. I don't know if it was a feminine narcissism, but it was the quality of an actor.

> MARQUIS CHILDS, political commentator

- Meeting Roosevelt was like sipping your first bottle of champagne.
- He died on the wings of victory, but he saw those wings and heard them beating [April 1945].

WINSTON CHURCHILL, British prime minister

- As far as radio is concerned, Roosevelt is a natural-born artist.
- He is a scab president leading a great scab army.

FATHER CHARLES E. COUGHLIN, pro-Fascist priest, demagogue, and anti-Semitic radio broadcaster

- He is a man who thinks the shortest distance between two points is not a straight line but a corkscrew.
- The president, in his ideas for programs, reminds me of a farmer with too many puppies. He took them out on a boat, dumped them overboard, and kept those that could swim back to shore.

ELMER DAVIS, radio commentator and journalist

- If he is the next president, he will serve with honor and credit to himself. He seems to have strength and equipoise with roundness of judgment and common sense.

CHARLES C. DAWES, vice president under Calvin Coolidge

- It was difficult to contradict this artist, this seducer.

CHARLES DE GAULLE, French general

JAMES C. HUMES

- Of course, Roosevelt had an Oedipus complex as big as a house.

    JOHN GUNTHER, American political commentator

- That Jew cripple.

    ADOLF HITLER, German führer

- Young Roosevelt knows nothing about finance, but he *doesn't* know he doesn't know.

    FRANKLIN LANE, secretary of the interior
    under President Woodrow Wilson

- Franklin Roosevelt is no crusader. He is no tribune of the people. He is no enemy of special privilege. He is a very pleasant man who without any important qualifications for office would very much like to be president [in 1932].

    WALTER LIPPMANN, journalist

- Roosevelt is a screech owl. A screech owl slips into the roost, scootches up to the hen, and talks softly to her. The hen falls in love with him, and the next thing you know, there is no hen.

    HUEY LONG, Louisiana senator and sometime
    national rival of FDR

- Franklin could be *so* charming. There are two things I didn't like about him—his face.
- FDR stands for Feather Duster Roosevelt [1932].
- The three demagogues—the Führer, Duce, and Roosevelt—FDR [1936].

> ALICE ROOSEVELT LONGWORTH, daughter of
> Theodore Roosevelt and cousin of Eleanor Roosevelt

- Each man has his signature gesture: Hitler with his raised hand of salute, Churchill with his V sign, and Roosevelt with his index finger pointing in the wind.

> CLARE BOOTHE LUCE, playwright
> and U.S. Republican representative

- Roosevelt will probably go down in American history as a great hero. It is one of our Heavenly Father's characteristic jokes upon the American people and in the usual bad taste.
- Roosevelt is one of the most charming of men, but like many another charming man, he leaves in the beholder the impression that he is also somewhat shallow and futile.

> H. L. MENCKEN, newspaper editor and columnist

- Roosevelt is an extraordinarily difficult person to describe . . .

weary as well as buoyant, frivolous as well as grave, evasive as well as frank . . . a man of bewildering complexity of moods and motives.

> HENRY MORGENTHAU Jr., secretary of the treasury

- Charming and remarkable, Roosevelt seemed like one of the great hostesses of Europe.

> SIR OSWALD MOSLEY, British fascist

- He was all right, but he was a bigot. He didn't like Tammany Hall. He didn't like poor people. He was a patronizing son of a bitch.

> DANIEL O'CONNELL, Albany Democratic party boss

- Roosevelt was the most complicated person I have ever known.
- He is guided by two ambitions—to outshine Al Smith and his cousin, Theodore.

> FRANCES PERKINS, secretary of labor

- He was never one of the boys, although he frequently made a good try. It was such a good try that it never quite came off.

> MIKE REILLY, chief of White House Secret Service detail

- He is the first Harvard man to know enough to avoid three syllables when he has something to say.

    WILL ROGERS, vaudevillian and humorist

- Franklin [Roosevelt] is nine-tenths mush and one-tenth Eleanor.

    EDITH CAROW ROOSEVELT, widow of Theodore Roosevelt

- I was one of those who served his purpose.
- Franklin finds it hard to relax with people who aren't his social equal.

    ELEANOR ROOSEVELT, wife of FDR

- Franklin is a fine fellow. I just wish he weren't a Democrat [in 1910].

    THEODORE ROOSEVELT, U.S. president and FDR's cousin

- His intellectual processes have always been intuitive rather than logical. He often thought lazily and superficially.

    ARTHUR SCHLESINGER JR., historian of the
    New Deal and Roosevelt biographer

- He was hard as well as soft. At times he displayed a capacity for vindictiveness, which could be described as petty, and at other times, he demonstrated the Christian spirit of forgiveness and charity in its purest form.

    ROBERT SHERWOOD, playwright and White House speechwriter

- He was the kindest man you ever met but just don't get in his way.

ALFRED E. SMITH, New York governor and
Democratic candidate for president

- Churchill would pick your pocket for a kopeck. Roosevelt is not like that. He dips in his hands for larger coins.

JOSEPH STALIN, Soviet dictator

- He was a cold, selfish S.O.B., but history will rate him as a great president.
- His voice is silent, but his courage is not spent [at FDR's death].

HARRY S. TRUMAN, U.S. president

- Roosevelt was, it cannot be emphasized too much, a child of the country.

REX TUGWELL, FDR brain truster

- He was a daring adventurer. . . . I reached the conclusion that I would under no circumstances ever have any business dealings with him.

HENRY WALLACE, vice president to FDR

- He was socially wonderful—truly he could charm birds off the trees—but he was more charming than able.

     EDITH WILSON, wife of President Woodrow Wilson

- He'll bear watching. I think he has a political future.

     WOODROW WILSON, U.S. president

FDR's Firsts

PERHAPS IT IS NOT surprising that Franklin D. Roosevelt, the longest-serving president, would be the U.S. chief executive who broke more precedents than any other in history. But it is also due to the nature of his presidency. He did not just preside over his country; he led. He also, by personality and inclination, was a risk taker.

At a time when it was not considered that "safe," he over-ruled his advisers and flew in a small plane from Albany, New York, to Chicago to accept the nomination for president by his party. When there was great political downside to appointing women to a high office, he named the first woman to a cabinet position.

This was FDR. He knew that "playing it safe" never won headlines, and Roosevelt knew how to make front-page news.

Bank Holiday

Roosevelt, as the newly sworn-in president, immediately after taking office in March 1933, issued an executive order shutting down and closing all the banks for business. In proclaiming "a bank holiday," he gave the Treasury Department time to devise measures to save the nation's banking system.

Bueno Viaje

Franklin Roosevelt was the first president to journey to South America. In December 1936, he sailed to Buenos Aires to preside over a conference of Latin American nations. At that time, it was the longest trip any president had ever taken. It was an outgrowth of his "Good Neighbor Policy."

Hitler's ascendancy and threat made Roosevelt even more eager to cement Latin American ties and to unite the Western Hemisphere against meddling by the Fascist leader.

Dutch Treat

Franklin Roosevelt is the only president to be sworn in at inaugural ceremonies with his hand over a Bible written in a foreign language. When he took the oath from Chief Justice Charles Evans Hughes in 1933, Roosevelt chose for the ceremony the

Roosevelt family Bible written in Dutch and dating back to 1702, which belonged to Jacobus Roosevelt, progenitor of the Hyde Park Roosevelts.

"Fair" Reception

Roosevelt was the first chief executive to deliver a speech on television. For the opening of the World's Fair in New York City on April 30, 1939, Roosevelt delivered his remarks from the Federal Building on the Egyptian grounds. The event was televised by NBC.

Fatal "Footnote"?

Franklin D. Roosevelt is the only president to unwittingly leave a portent of his impending death. As he slumped to his death from a fatal stroke in Warm Springs, Georgia, on April 14, 1945, the mystery novel he was reading fell from his lap to his feet. It was Carter Dickson's *The Punch and Judy Murders*, and it was opened to page 28 at the beginning of a chapter entitled "Six Feet of Earth."

"Ferdinand Magellan"

Roosevelt was the first president to have his own special presidential car designed to be attached to a train. The car was built in 1938 and was reinforced with steel, bulletproof glass, and wide aisles so that the crippled president could navigate it with a wheelchair. It was christened *Ferdinand Magellan*. President Truman would also use it to take Churchill to deliver his Iron Curtain speech in 1946, and two years later it was the vehicle for Truman's "Give 'em hell, folks" presidential campaign for his upset victory in 1948.

Fishy Business

Roosevelt is the only president in White House history to insist on fish for his daily breakfast fare. The frequent yachtsman and former assistant secretary of the navy said that he preferred "sailor's fare," which consisted of cod, mackerel, and herring.

Flying Franklin!

Franklin D. Roosevelt was the first presidential candidate to have a plane fly him to a convention to deliver his acceptance speech. On July 2, 1932, Governor Roosevelt flew from Albany, New York, to Chicago, Illinois, to accept the Democratic Party nomination for president. The dramatic flight said more than the speech that followed. It signaled that Roosevelt was a man who would act fast in meeting the challenge of the Depression.

Frances the First

Roosevelt was the first chief executive to appoint a woman to the cabinet. Frances Perkins was named secretary of labor in 1933. She had served under Governor Roosevelt in Albany, New York, in a similar position, and she was the only cabinet member to last throughout all the years of his presidency. Organized labor had vigorously opposed her appointment in 1933. Perkins asked Roosevelt how he took the five days of protests by top labor officials. "Easier than the five years of nagging that I would have taken from you if I had withdrawn your name," replied Roosevelt.

"The Godfather"

Roosevelt was the first president to be godfather of a child of the British royal family. In 1942, the Duke of Kent, the younger brother of King George VI, served as proxy for Roosevelt's role as spiritual sponsor of his son, Michael George Charles Franklin. The ceremony took place July 4, 1942. As an Episcopalian, Roosevelt was a fellow communicant of the Anglican Duke of Kent. Roosevelt's godson, Prince Michael, is a first cousin of Queen Elizabeth II. His father, the Duke of Kent, would die later that year when his plane was shot down over Europe by the Germans.

"High Five"

Franklin D. Roosevelt was the first chief executive to win electoral votes for president and vice president five times. These were contests for the two highest nationally elected offices of the nation. Most are familiar with his four winning contests for the presidency—the first in 1932 against Hoover, the fourth against Dewey in 1944. Less well known is his losing race for vice president in 1920, when he ran with newspaper editor Governor James Cox of Ohio against Warren Harding and Calvin Coolidge. Though he lost, Roosevelt established himself as a national figure in the Democratic Party.

(Interestingly, Richard Nixon also would later win votes for the two top national offices—five times—twice as vice president with Dwight Eisenhower in 1952 and 1956. Then he waged his losing race against John Kennedy in 1960. Following that was his win in 1968 and his reelection in 1972.)

"Hooray for Hollywood!"

Roosevelt was the first and only chief executive to have written a film script for Hollywood. While Roosevelt was recovering from polio in 1922, the former assistant secretary of the navy wrote a movie script about the *U.S.S. Constitution*, nicknamed "Old Ironsides," America's most venerable ship.

JAMES C. HUMES

Inauguration Innovation

Franklin D. Roosevelt was the first president to be inaugurated in January instead of March. The House of Representatives became controlled by Democrats in the elections of 1930 following the stock market crash of 1929. There was a drive for the Twentieth Amendment to the Constitution, which would push back the inauguration date from March to January. In the twentieth century, there was no need for the later date since trains and cars had replaced the horse and buggy. Sensing a Democratic victory in the presidency in 1932, Governor Roosevelt and other leading Democrats urged the change. Accordingly, on January 20, 1937, the reelected Roosevelt took his inaugural oath instead of in March.

"The King and I"

Roosevelt was the first president to host the British royal family at the White House. In June 1941, as Britain, alone, faced the onslaught of Hitler in Europe, Roosevelt, though the United States maintained its neutrality, opened the doors of the White House to King George VI and his wife, Queen Elizabeth, as a symbolic gesture of sympathy.

The royal couple had journeyed down by train from Ottawa,

Canada, to stay with the Roosevelts at Hyde Park, and then they all went to Washington, D.C.

King Franklin I

Roosevelt won four presidential elections—against President Hoover in 1932, Governor Alfred Landon of Kansas in 1936, utilities executive Wendell Willkie in 1940, and Governor Thomas Dewey of New York in 1944.

The two-term tradition had been an iron precedent ever since George Washington refused to run again in 1796. In his decision to run for a third term, Roosevelt likened his situation to being conscripted for military service to continue as commander in chief as the danger of war threatened.

In 1944, he would then run a fourth term, which ended, like the reign of a monarch, only with his death.

Like Father, Like Son

Roosevelt was the first president to appoint a son to the same position his father held—secretary of agriculture. Roosevelt named Henry Wallace Jr. in 1933 to the same position his father, Henry Wallace Sr., held under Calvin Coolidge. The Wallace family published an agricultural magazine out of Iowa. The younger

Wallace was a Democrat, unlike his Republican father. He became popular with the left wing of the Democratic Party. Roosevelt made him his running mate in 1940. Then four years later, conservative forces from the South and elsewhere forced Wallace off the ticket, and Harry Truman was nominated for vice president. In 1948 Wallace was the Progressive Party candidate against President Truman. The Communist Party in the United States would back Wallace.

Loyal Opposition

Roosevelt was the first chief executive to appoint leading members of the opposing party to head top positions in his cabinet. In 1941, after Roosevelt had been elected to an unprecedented third term, he named Henry Stimson to be secretary of war and Col. Frank Knox to be secretary of the navy. Stimson had been secretary of state for Herbert Hoover, Roosevelt's predecessor, and Knox had been the Republican Party candidate for vice president, running with Governor Alfred Landon in 1936. It created a semblance of bipartisanship in U.S. foreign policy as Britain was fighting Hitler alone in World War II.

"Meet the Press"

Roosevelt was the first president to hold regular sessions with the press. His cousin, Theodore Roosevelt, introduced the practice of occasionally meeting with reporters. Before Franklin Roosevelt, his predecessors Coolidge and Hoover would occasionally deliver answers to prepared submitted questions.

Franklin Roosevelt, however, instituted informal questioning by journalists, to which he would give on-the-spot replies. It was far from the adversarial encounters seen today.

First, the press, for the most part, was warm to the engaging president and sympathetic to his policies. Second, they were grateful for this source of news.

Merci, Monsieur President

Roosevelt was the first president to deliver a speech in a foreign language to citizens of another country. From Quebec City in Canada, on August 7, 1943, Roosevelt addressed the citizens of the small islands of Sainte-Pierre and Miquelon in Newfoundland Bay. Officially, they were part of Vichy, France, which was then a puppet state of Germany. The five thousand or so citizens, however, had transferred their allegiance to the Free French led by General de Gaulle in exile in London. In giving the address, FDR overrode the opposition of his own State Department.

Miami Mayhem

Roosevelt is the first president-elect to be shot at in an assassination attempt. On February 14, 1933, the already elected Roosevelt was in Miami following a pre-inaugural vacation cruise in the Bahamas on the yacht of Vincent Astor. An anarchist, Giuseppe Zangara, fired a shot at Roosevelt. It hit Mayor Anton Cermak of Chicago, Illinois, who was in the limousine discussing federal plans that might aid his city. Cermak was killed, and Zangara ("I don't hate Roosevelt. I hate all in authority.") was later executed. The constitution amendment pushing up the inauguration to January was finally ratified in November of that year.

(History reports there were rumors of a plot against Abraham Lincoln in February 1861, and Lincoln, accordingly, was sneaked into the capital city from Baltimore in the dead of night.)

Monitoring or Meddling?

President Roosevelt authorized monitoring the telephone traffic by those of German ancestry to the fatherland. In 1940 the Bund, a pro-Nazi German-American group, was active in

Yorkville, a section in New York City, where many German-speaking U.S. citizens of Teutonic descent lived. (*The House on 92nd Street*, a 1945 espionage thriller film, was based on subversive activities centered in this area.)

At a time when President George W. Bush is attacked for monitoring the Mideast destinations of telephone calls made by Arab-Americans overseas, Roosevelt's surveillance operation during the years before World War II is noteworthy.

No Capitol Ceremony!

For the first and only time in presidential history, a Washington inauguration ceremony in 1945 was held at the White House and not on the steps of the U.S. Capitol. It was the first wartime inaugural since Abraham Lincoln's in 1865.

After his reelection in 1944, an ailing and weary president delivered the shortest inaugural address in history on the portico of the White House.

"Over There"

Roosevelt was the first commander in chief to travel in wartime out of the country. He flew to Morocco in 1942 to meet Prime Minister Churchill and General Eisenhower. The next December he went to Teheran for his first visit with Marshal Stalin, as well as with Churchill. Then in 1945, Roosevelt also conferred with Churchill and Stalin at the momentous Yalta Conference. (Also worth mentioning is Roosevelt's over-the-border trip to Quebec City, Canada, in August of 1943.)

Philatelist President

Franklin Delano Roosevelt is the only president whose principal hobby was stamp collecting. As a youth, he was fascinated with faraway places. The Delanos on his mother's side had made a fortune in their clipper-ship trade to China. His collection increased through his Harvard days and his time as assistant secretary of the navy. As president, he received stamps from kings and heads of state—prized first-release stamps. After his death, America's largest stamp collection was sold at a worth of close to $200,000.

Roosevelt the Repressor?

Franklin Roosevelt holds the dubious distinction of being the only chief executive to order close to one hundred thousand U.S. citizens to be transported to detention camps. In his executive order as commander in chief in February 1942, he placed U.S.

citizens of Japanese descent in military guarded "centers" in Utah. Interestingly, J. Edgar Hoover, the FBI. director, opposed the internment. The *Washington Post*, in its editorial denunciation of the policy, compared it to Hitler's putting Jews in concentration camps.

Spell It Out!

Franklin Roosevelt, in his first inaugural in March 1933, insisted on repeating all the oath words that Chief Justice Charles Evans Hughes read out instead of just saying "I do" to the questions posed by the chief justice. Roosevelt recited in full the words "support the Constitution of the United States . . ." and the words of oath that followed. Succeeding presidents have followed FDR's innovation.

The Two Roosevelts

Franklin Roosevelt's ascension to the White House would make his New Amsterdam Dutch surname the longest presiding name in American history—and all in the twentieth century. Theodore Roosevelt presided from the date in September 1900, when he became chief executive upon President McKinley's death until he left the presidency in March 1909. Then his distant cousin Franklin, who was inaugurated in March 1933, would serve until his death in April 1945.

In between those years, ex-president Theodore Roosevelt dominated the news with his world tour following his presidential years and then his presidential run in 1912 on the Progressive Party ticket. In his defeat by Wilson, his cousin Franklin would edge into national politics by his serving as President Wilson's assistant secretary of the navy and then running for vice president in 1920.

It is hard to imagine Franklin Roosevelt ever becoming president if Theodore had not preceded him. The younger Roosevelt chose politics against his mother's wishes because of Theodore's success and prominence. The handsome Franklin no doubt sought the homely Eleanor's hand because her uncle was president.

Without that famous name, the Democrat Franklin would not have won the state senate seat in 1910 that had long been a safe Republican bastion.

And then when Democrat Wilson was elected, young Roosevelt lobbied to be assistant secretary of the navy, a post in which his cousin Theodore had gained fame. Again in 1920, the former assistant secretary of the navy was picked to run for vice president because of his vote-winning last name. His cousin Theodore had died a year before.

Then, when Franklin became president, he chose "New Deal" to be the name of his progressive policies in imitation of Theodore Roosevelt's "Square Deal."

Way Before Watergate

In 1940 President Roosevelt had a recording device placed in the Oval Office. For this surveillance activity, he asked General Roy Sarnoff of Radio Corporation of America (RCA) to do the installation. Roosevelt had been perturbed by leaks of confidential information that had been given to senators in private meetings at the White House.

Swearing In at the White House

Roosevelt was the chief executive who established the precedent of having cabinet officials sworn in at the White House before their family and friends. Before Roosevelt, they were sworn in by a minor official of the chief executive in their department, not by the president. Now, the president personally swears them in.

FDR's Fables

FRANKLIN ROOSEVELT WAS THE greatest raconteur in the White House between the presidencies of Abraham Lincoln and Ronald Reagan. Like them, he was a superb mimic with a professional comic's sense of timing. In addition, like those other chief executives, he could laugh at himself. Roosevelt relished the chance to tell stories at his own expense.

It is true that in the anecdotes that follow we do not find the bons mots or witty rejoinders of Winston Churchill. Partially that is because facile wordplay and turning an opponent's words to your own advantage are honed in the daily jousting in the House of Commons. By its rules, members of Parliament are not allowed to read from prepared scripts. American chief executives, even those who have served in Congress, have not developed the art of repartee. Yet in one display of humor, politicians on this side of the Atlantic are superior to their British counterparts. Americans are better raconteurs, having polished the skills of mimicry and timing in their retelling of their favorite anecdotes.

The stories that follow are a testament to Roosevelt's high humor and insouciant personality. It is hard not to develop an affection for the infectious FDR personality after reading them.

If some of the anecdotes are apocryphal and cannot be authenticated, it is useful to keep in mind FDR's comments, "Let a good story ride because the truth will eventually take care of itself."

Baby Blessing

Master Franklin was not yet four when the family visited Washington, D.C. In 1886 James Roosevelt of Hyde Park took his son to see President Grover Cleveland at the White House. Roosevelt had met Cleveland in Albany, New York, when he was governor.

Cleveland placed his hand in the little boy's hand and said, "I'm making a strange wish for you, little man—a wish that no one else would make."

The president then said, "I pray that you may never be president of the United States."

Barkin' Up the Wrong Tree?

In 1938 FDR tried to enact his court-packing legislation to ex-
pand the number of the Supreme Court membership. Its purpose was to dilute the conservative majority, which was blocking
some New Deal programs. The bill was controversial, and even
the staunchest of his Democratic allies were sensing resistance
by voters. Roosevelt's vice president, John Nance Garner, was
asked to make some soundings. The bourbon-belting, tobacco-
chewing former Speaker of the House, known as Cactus Jack,
was called into the office by FDR.

Garner said, "Captain, do you want it with the bark on or
off?"

"Off," said the president. "It's a dog that won't hunt."

Basic Needs?

The first meeting of President Roosevelt and Prime Minister
Churchill took place in Newfoundland Bay in August 1941. FDR
brought with him a draft that would declare a common ground
of ideals for the two democratic nations.

Roosevelt broached his idea of Four Freedoms—Freedom of
Speech, Freedom of Religion, Freedom from Fear, and another
Freedom—"Four" was more alliterative with Freedom, and there

was another basic need to be met. He considered "Freedom from Hunger," but that was too narrow—it did not cover the basics of shelter and clothing. So he came up with "Freedom from Want." But when he mentioned it to Churchill, the prime minister responded, "Just make sure 'Freedom from Want' does not mean 'Freedom from Desire.' That's also a basic need."

"The Best Gifts Come in Small Packages"

When the Yalta Conference with Churchill and Stalin ended in February 1945, FDR boarded the destroyer *Murphy* to sail to Cairo to visit King Farouk en route home. In Cairo, King Ibn Saud, the Bedouin monarch, came aboard.

Roosevelt, in line with the Arab custom of exchanging gifts, told Saud he would be sending him a Douglas aircraft complete with crew. Yet Saud, who had brought for Roosevelt a gold scimitar, a leather saddle, and a chieftain's ornate costume, seemed a bit miffed that the president had no gifts at that time for Saud to open.

Admiral McIntyre, FDR's physician, came to the rescue. "The president wanted you to have these magic potions," he said, and he placed two vials before the king. "It is called penicillin." Ibn Saud's doctor then asked, "Does it cure syphilis?"

"Yes," said McIntyre. King Saud beamed his satisfaction when informed by his doctor.

Bicycle Built for Five

Soon after it was learned that Governor Roosevelt had been nominated by the Democratic National Convention in Chicago in July 1932, as the party's presidential candidate, a three-motored plane was sighted in the Albany, New York, airport. Reporters asked if FDR was going to use the plane to fly to Chicago.

Roosevelt answered, "Now I'll tell you what I'm going to do. . . . I'm going to bicycle to Chicago. I'm going to get one of those 'quinters'—you know—that have five riders on a bicycle.

"I'll ride in the first seat and manage the handlebars. James will ride the second, then Elliott, then Franklin Jr., and then John. Sam [referring to speechwriter and aide New York Supreme Court Justice Samuel Rosenman] will follow on a tricycle."

Body Odor

When Harry Hopkins, FDR's top personal adviser was visiting London in 1942, it was reported that Pierre Laval, the foremost French Nazi, was being appointed premier by the aging figurehead Marshal Petain in the Vichy government. That decision affirmed the status of France as a puppet nation under Hitler.

Hopkins cabled Roosevelt, "How about nailing that wood pussy [skunk] Laval to your barn door?"

Roosevelt replied, "Your suggestion is being studied, but the consensus of opinion is that the odor is still too strong for a family of nations."

The Book of Ruth?

In 1920, while Franklin Roosevelt was assistant secretary of the navy, he was—partly because of the name of former President Theodore Roosevelt, who died the year before—selected to be the vice presidential Democratic candidate to run with Governor James Cox of Ohio. Roosevelt would do most of the campaigning. Warren Harding, the Republican candidate, was expected to win.

In October, Roosevelt boarded a train from New York City bound for Rochester—the first upstate city in a series of campaign stops. When the train arrived at the Rochester Station in late morning, Roosevelt was met in his compartment by railroad security officers, who ushered him out on a cordoned route away from the station.

A puzzled Roosevelt asked, "Why the special security precautions?"

"There are huge crowds for Ruth."

"Roosevelt, did you say? Why that's a wonderful election sign," said Roosevelt.

The security man answered, "They're not for you. They're here to see Babe Ruth arrive. Ruth is booked to play an exhibition game this afternoon." The Yankee home run phenomenon was on a barnstorming tour with the Yankees and players from other teams.

Border Belt?

FDR loved regaling White House visitors about his experiences campaigning for the New York state senate. One late afternoon he was both tired and thirsty after making many town stops in the rural upstate farming constituency of Dutchess County. He parked his Maxwell roadster in front of a tavern. Pulling himself up to the counter, he told the bartender, "Drinks for everyone in the house." Everyone took his glass of beer, and Roosevelt announced, "I'm Franklin Roosevelt trying to go to Albany for the state senate seat."

"Don't you mean Hartford?" said one of the imbibers at the bar. "This is Sharon, Connecticut."

"Button, Button, Who's Got the Button?"

As the year 1944 rolled in, the tide in World War II had begun to shift against the Axis. After their losses in the Battle of Midway, the Japanese were fighting a defensive war. But 1944 was also a presidential election year, and one name figured prominently in speculations. Republicans were entertaining the idea of running the heroic and popular General Douglas MacArthur against the current president, FDR.

In the spring, MacArthur and Admiral Chester Nimitz were called to a meeting in Hawaii to settle differences between the army and navy in strategic priorities and first objectives (such as the Philippines, to which MacArthur had promised to return).

FDR called the general aside and said, "General, it is my honor to present an award no commander in chief has ever given to a general officer on the field." MacArthur glowed as the president handed over a small case and directed MacArthur to open it. The general did and found, to his chagrin, a campaign button emblazoned "MAC FOR PRESIDENT."

By George!

During World War I, when David Lloyd George became the British prime minister in a new wartime coalition government, he selected the opposition Conservative Party leader, Arthur Balfour, as foreign secretary.

When America entered the war, Balfour was sent over to the United States to discuss strategy with Britain's new ally. One Sunday, the assistant secretary of the navy took Balfour to see the sights, including Mount Vernon. Roosevelt said, "This is the Potomac, where George Washington supposedly threw a silver dollar across. Of course, it's not really true—it's apocryphal."

Balfour replied, "Why not? Didn't he throw a sovereign across the Atlantic Ocean?"

The Chief "Chickens" Out

Since the inauguration ceremony in 1945 was to take place at the White House and not the Capitol, the official festivities would be limited to that location. FDR requested his favorite dish for the two thousand who would be attending: "chicken à la king."

After the shortest inaugural address in history, FDR said informally, "Now on this cold January day, we can all have some hot chicken à la king."

Yet, on the menu passed out, chicken à la king was listed, but only cold chicken salad was offered.

The chief executive remonstrated with his chief chef, Mrs. Henrietta Nesbitt, who replied "You may be the president, but there is no way I can keep chicken à la king hot for all those people."

The big headline the next day was not his message but his menu: "HOUSEKEEPER VETOES FDR ON HIS MENU."

Clean Out of Ideas?

In early 1941, President Roosevelt invited his former opponent Wendell Willkie to visit the White House. (Willkie would afterward visit Prime Minister Churchill carrying the president's best wishes, including a poem by Longfellow handwritten by FDR, "Sail on O Ship of State . . .")

When Roosevelt's secretary Missy LeHand reported to the president that Willkie was on his way in, FDR noted that his desk was empty of papers.

Roosevelt said, "Missy, roll the table over there or even the trash basket for some papers to put on my desk. A clean desk means an empty mind, Missy."

Cold Shoulder

During the war, a reporter asked the president if the ban on parking on highways (as part of the World War II internal defense program) included the shoulders next to the defense highways.

"You mean parking shoulders?" Roosevelt asked.

"Yes. Forbidding to let the civilians park if the military should have to use them."

Roosevelt retorted, "We're never going to ban good necking places in this administration."

Comedy of Manners?

In 1943, during World War II, Madame Chiang Kai-shek, wife of the Chinese republic's generalissimo, visited the Roosevelts at the White House. The self-styled "First Lady of the Orient" was always well aware of her sensuous effect upon men as she would slither across the room in her slit trousers. Privately, Mrs. Roosevelt used to refer to her as "the Dragon Lady." Madame Chiang Kai-shek once suggested to FDR how she would handle the recalcitrant labor leader John L. Lewis by stroking her fingers across the front of her neck.

Following dinner and drinks in the study, Madame Chiang Kai-shek coyly made her leave, saying to the wheelchaired president, "You needn't get up."

Roosevelt replied, "Madame, I couldn't even if I had to."

Cool-Aid?

In 1924, Calvin Coolidge, who had succeeded to the presidency the year before on the death of Warren Harding, won election in a landslide that was propelled in part by the campaign slogan "Keep Cool with Coolidge." The laconic and phlegmatic New Englander seemed to be a popular contrast to the freneticism of the twenties as the economy soared.

Yet Roosevelt sensed there was another part of America that was not sharing in the expanding wealth.

To the New York State Democratic Convention in 1926, in a speech nominating Robert Wagner for senator, Roosevelt drew the audience to their feet, saying, "The people of the East have learned, through months of struggle to get coal for their furnaces and stoves, the hard meaning of the slogan 'Keep Cool with Coolidge.'"

Covering All Bets

In 1930, as the Great Crash was followed by the Depression, the political world sensed that President Hoover would not win reelection. The Democratic nomination to oppose him was a very desirable position to be in. Governor of New York, Franklin Roosevelt, was the leading candidate, if he could tie down his states' delegates, many of whom were still loyal to the previous governor, 1928 Democratic candidate Al Smith.

Jim Farley, the Irish Catholic head of the Elks Lodge nationally, and Sam Rosenman, FDR's chief assistant, along with Louis Howe, scurried across New York state trying to nail down delegates. Howe was the driver. Howe, whose sloppy appearance was only exceeded by his careless driving, kept his passenger's nails bitten to the raw. On one sliding turn, the Catholic Farley could see the Jewish Rosenman crossing himself.

FDR, in telling the story, would add, "Sam was just covering himself with every faith."

Cover Up

Shortly after the polio-stricken Franklin Roosevelt settled in for a long stay at Warm Springs, Georgia, for its healing waters, the pastor of the community's largest Baptist church called one late afternoon on its distinguished New York visitor.

When the good reverend's words, "I have come to offer 'spiritual comfort,'" resonated from the doorway to Roosevelt, Missy LeHand, his secretary, quickly spread a tablecloth over another kind of "spiritual comfort" in the form of a cocktail shaker and glasses. She knew Roosevelt would not want the leading cleric in this, Georgia's driest county in this era of Prohibition, to know that her boss also might immerse himself in the bracing warmth of other liquids.

Crazy Chameleon

In the 1940 presidential campaign, Roosevelt poked fun at the Republican Party for its inconsistencies and contradictory policies.

"Its various positions require a contortionist. If one would try to find a common color, he'd go nuts. It would be like the chameleon bug who went crazy after it landed itself on a Scottish tartan."

A Crimson-Faced College President

In the fall of 1900, an eighteen-year-old Franklin Roosevelt graduated from Groton School to enter Harvard. The tall and slender Roosevelt, at one hundred fifty pounds, had too slight a frame for football. So he concentrated his energies as a "compet" for the *Harvard Crimson*, the school newspaper. That fall, President William McKinley was running for reelection against William Jennings Bryan. Even though his distant cousin, Governor Theodore Roosevelt, was the Republican vice presidential candidate paired with McKinley, Roosevelt maintained the Democratic convictions of the Hyde Park branch of the family. (His meeting of Theodore's niece, Eleanor, was still years in the future.) But from his mother's friends in the summer, he had gathered that Charles W. Eliot, president of Harvard at that time, had supported McKinley four years earlier in 1896 and was likely to do so again, even though it was a tradition for Harvard presidents to remain neutral.

Roosevelt visited the president's office on a campus matter but tricked Eliot into admitting he was for McKinley. Roosevelt then published his "interview" with Eliot, revealing the president's endorsement of McKinley. It was picked up by national newspapers.

A furious Eliot told Roosevelt, "You deceived me and violated university precepts." The scoop helped propel Roosevelt to be the president of the *Crimson* in his second year at Harvard.

"Cwazy—You're Driving Me Cwazy!"
Senator Cordell Hull from Tennessee declared his support for Governor Roosevelt for president early on in 1932. The distinguished legislator was known for his low tariff views and support for Wilson's League of Nations. Roosevelt appointed him secretary of state, but the president was closer to his fellow Grotonian Sumner Welles, whom he made undersecretary of state, much to Hull's dismay. The pontifical Hull did not gibe well with FDR. The Tennesseean's trouble with the letter R did nothing to ease the clash in temperaments. In particular, Hull's oath, "For Cwist's sake," which was spoken in an argument, rubbed raw the president's nerves.

FDR said to his secretary Missy LeHand, "Why, he can't even curse like a man. If he says 'for Cwist's sake' again, I'm going to 'scweam' back at him and add, 'What you're saying is 'wotten wubbish.'"

Derrière Déjà Vu

Fanny Hurst was a bestselling novelist of the 1930s. The Rubenesque writer was a favorite of FDR because of her wit and lusty good humor. After a crash diet, the New York author phoned to say she was coming up to Hyde Park for a visit.

When told the president was in the library, she announced as she was entering, "Close your eyes, Franklin. I have a surprise. Now open."

She pirouetted and turned to hear the president say, "Different Hurst but same old 'fanny.'"

Diapers and a Drunk

In 1940, as FDR inched his way toward announcing a third term, he watched with amused eye the announcements of various Democrats and Republicans hopeful of succeeding him in the White House. One of these for the Republicans was thirty-eight-year-old New York City prosecutor Thomas Dewey. The other one was his retiring vice president, "Cactus Jack" Garner from Texas, who regularly kept company with another Jack with the last name of Daniel.

"I thought," said FDR, "the days of 'wet' and 'dry' candidates were over at the repeal of Prohibition. But I see announcing themselves are two—one who has thrown his diaper into the ring, and the other one who hasn't been weaned from his bottle."

Due Recognition?

The president relished recounting this experience from his gubernatorial days, which he often did after an introduction for which he had received a warm welcome. "It's always gratifying to my office being given its proper recognition. I remember once, while governor, when I was making an inspection tour of a mental hospital. A worker landscaping the front grounds, upon seeing the limousine, made obeisance with a courtly deep bow. As we pulled out of range, I looked back and the same person was rendering me the four-fingered salute from his nose."

"The Face of God"

Franklin Roosevelt, despite the burdens of office and his affliction of paralysis, just about always managed to maintain his high humor. He did not like to dwell on unpleasant things. He left visits to hospitals to his wife. On one particular occasion, he himself had to be the bearer of bad news. Through Prime Minister Churchill on December 11, 1941, he learned that an American pilot, John Gillespie Magee Jr., had been shot down over Germany. Roosevelt knew the young man. His father, Reverend John Gillespie Magee Sr., was the rector of St. John's Episcopal Church in Lafayette Square across from the White House. His son—before the United States had entered the war—had enlisted in the Canadian Royal Air Force (RAF).

Roosevelt telephoned his friend, the rector. A few days later Magee delivered by hand to the White House the poem "High Flight" that he had received from his aviator son after his reported death.

Some of the words, which President Reagan would later quote in his tribute to the crashed *Challenger* spacecraft, may be familiar:

> *Up, up the long delirious burning blue,*
> *I've topped the wind-swept heights with easy grace*
> *Where never lark, nor even eagle flew—*
> *And, while with silent lifting mind I've trod*

The high untrespassed sanctity of space,
Put out my hand and touched the face of God.

Family Values?

In 1928 Governor Al Smith of New York was nominated by the Democrats to run against Herbert Hoover for the White House. In turn, Smith pressured Roosevelt to run to succeed him as governor in order to help ensure that New York would be safely in the Democratic column in November. Smith's Catholicism was a liability to Protestant Democratic voters. Some of the dimmer sort actually believed Smith would, at the pope's order, make America Catholic!

One questioner at a Democratic rally in New York said, "Will Al Smith's election make my Protestant marriage illegal and my children illegitimate?"

"I can tell you that, as long as I'm governor, my five children and yours will never become bastards."

Fare-Thee-Better?

Historians may differ on the choice of the worst president, but if food critics had to pick the worst presidential chef, they might well name Henrietta Nesbitt, who was the maestro of menus in the Roosevelt White House. If her drab diet exasperated the president, it perfectly suited Mrs. Roosevelt. "Simple, plain, and overcooked" was the former Albany housekeeper's recipe motto, whose meat entrees ran the gamut from boiled to chipped beef.

When FDR and his daughter, Anna, were supping together upstairs in the residence in 1944, Anna asked, "Tell me one good reason why you're running again."

"To fire Mrs. Nesbitt" was her father's answer.

FDR's Fantasy Film

William Randolph Hearst backed Roosevelt in 1932. The media mogul thought the dire times demanded a dictator. Hearst even financed a film on how a benevolent dictator could save the nation.

The presidential character, which was to be played by film star Walter Huston, has an automobile accident that puts him in a coma. The archangel Gabriel visits the stricken president in his stupor and tells him what to do.

Awakening, the chief executive establishes an army of construction. He invokes martial law, even ordering the execution of his enemies by a firing squad in front of the Statue of Liberty.

Hearst sent FDR the script. During his first week as president,

Roosevelt spent time revising it. He applauded the idea of the film, *Gabriel Over the White House*. The movie was one of the most popular films in the thirties. It came out in December 1933.

Fine-Tuning

Whenever a politician came calling on the president with a personal agenda, the particular proposal was deflected by the Rooseveltian charm.

Senator Huey Long advanced his populist national health scheme. FDR flashed his jaunty grin and said, "Fine, fine."

A little later, Vice President Jack Garner asked the president to veto some of the public works spending measures to balance the budget. The president again beamingly nodded, "Fine, fine."

But visitors never came away with any commitment, only the sweet-sounding word of "fine."

First Things First

In 1940 the comedy duo Abbott and Costello introduced their skit "Who's on First?" in a movie titled *One Night in the Tropics*. It set the nation howling, including the president.

One day, a long and complicated memorandum came to

Roosevelt's desk from the Department of the Treasury about the Federal Reserve.

Roosevelt attempted to read the memo, hoping to discover what was at issue and where the final responsibility for the regulations lay. He finally questioned Treasury Secretary Morgenthau, saying, "Who's on first?"

Fishing Fiasco

In August 1945, President Roosevelt met Prime Minister Winston Churchill in a historic conference at Quebec, Canada. Afterward, the two heads of government rode south on a train for a weekend rest at Hyde Park, the Roosevelt home on the Hudson River, eighty-five miles north of New York City. On a Saturday afternoon, the two went angling on a small lake nearby. Three hours of fishing netted frugal gain. Churchill landed only a little carp, but it ranked as colossal against the cipher of Roosevelt's results.

Afterward, Churchill asked the name of this unprofitable pond.

Roosevelt replied, "I don't know, but hereafter I will call it 'One Lake.'"

Front Page

FDR was a superb raconteur and mimic who relished stories that were directed against himself. One of his favorites was about the Union League Club in Philadelphia, a bastion of old Main Line families and hard-line Republicans. (The day after FDR's reelection in 1936, the Irish Democrat Jack Kelly, father of actress Grace Kelly, went up the Broad Street steps of the club and relieved himself.)

As FDR told the story, a member had moved to live in the club after the death of his wife. Every morning, at six thirty, he would walk down the steps and out of the club, go to the news vendor only a few yards away, slam a dollar into the paper seller's hand for the *Philadelphia Inquirer*, look at the front page, and then throw it down disgustedly and walk away.

After months, the vendor finally asked, "What are you looking for, sir?"

"An obituary" was the reply.

"Well, you don't find obituaries on the front page."

"You do if the obituary is of the S.O.B. I'm looking for."

Fuss Budget?

When her husband was governor of New York, Eleanor Roosevelt one day brought two Vassar College students from nearby Poughkeepsie over for lunch at Hyde Park.

One of the earnest young women asked the question, "What about the budget?"

Sara Delano Roosevelt, her mother-in-law, replied, "What budget? Franklin knows nothing about the budget."

The real mistress of Hyde Park elaborated, "I handle all matters of the budget!"

"Grin and Bare It"

In 1910 the twenty-eight-year-old Franklin Roosevelt announced his candidacy for the state senate. In the strong Republican farming area of Dutchess County, New York, Roosevelt had two assets—his energy and his name. Theodore Roosevelt, who had left the White House the year before, was the most popular president in years.

In his campaign, Franklin emulated his cousin Theodore's ways and words. Everything was "bully" or "dee-lightful"—a dee-lightful day, dee-lightful weather, dee-lightful prospects.

But after one appearance, a young boy was skeptical.

"You're not the real Teddy," he said.

"How do you know that, young man?"

"Because you don't bare your teeth."

Gunboat Diplomacy

For his campaign for vice president in 1920, Franklin Roosevelt, still assistant secretary of the navy, tossed off this comment in Montana while defending the League of Nations. To the charge that Britain had six other dominions that would vote her way, Roosevelt replied, "Does anyone suppose that the votes of Cuba, Haiti, Santo Domingo, Panama, Nicaragua, and other Central American states would be cast differently from the United States? We are, in a very real sense, the big brother of those little republics."

And then he added, "You know, I have had something to do with running a couple of little republics. The facts are that I wrote Haiti's constitution myself, and if I do say so myself, I think it's a pretty good constitution."

The remarks drew great applause, and he repeated himself on the next two stops. Actually, Roosevelt hadn't written the constitution much less run a country, but it triggered a telling reply from Senator Harding, the Republican presidential nominee.

"I will not empower an assistant secretary of the navy to draft a constitution for helpless neighbors in the West Indies and jam it down their throats at the point of bayonets borne by the U.S. Marines."

Hail to Yale!

As assistant secretary of the navy, Roosevelt took the train up to Harvard for his tenth reunion, where he had been elected class marshal for the festivities. As the train from New York stopped at New Haven on the way to Boston, Roosevelt regaled his fellow passengers of his roommate's father, Lathrop Brown, whose love of Harvard and hatred of Yale knew no bounds.

Once, while coming up from New York City to Boston, Roosevelt had witnessed Brown ordering his three sons to disembark from the train when it stopped at New Haven so he and his sons could spit on the platform.

"Happy Days Are Here Again"

In June 1941, Franklin Delano Roosevelt Jr. married Margaret Dupont in Wilmington, Delaware. Although the day began sunny, a thundering cloudburst descended upon the wedding reception as if in judgment of this portentous union between the daughter of a corporate captain of capitalism and the son of the head of the Democratic Party.

A reporter asked the president if the rain burst had dimmed the spirits of the celebrants. FDR replied, "It's always a happy day when I see so many rich getting soaked."

Happy Hour?

FDR savored his "happy hour" at the White House. Six o'clock was the time when he would begin to mix cocktails for himself and a few of his friends or close aides. If he limited himself to only two drinks, the hour would often stretch more than sixty minutes. In his own family, only one would join him, "Sissy," as Anna the oldest daughter was called. When war came, his four sons were off serving in uniform.

If Sissy found out from his secretary that nobody else would be around at six o'clock, she would sometimes tuck a martini shaker in her bra and, unbeknownst to her mother (who disapproved of the drinking sessions because her father had died of alcoholism), slip into the Oval Office, not only with gin but with an array of gossip tidbits and risqué stories.

Anna told her daughter of one time when she heard her mother's voice approaching in the distance. Down went the shaker and glasses under the desk as Mrs. Roosevelt, in her high voice, said, "Franklin, I do wish you would read this memorandum on the poor coal miners."

The president would then have to return to the burdens of office.

Heavy Lifting

During World War II, the Office of Price Administration (OPA) became a bureaucratic leviathan regulating prices of such staples as sugar, butter, and gasoline.

When the bill proposing it was being drafted, FDR called in the head of OPA, Leon Henderson. "Leon, what about the constitutionality of this legislation and why isn't the Department of Labor included?"

Henderson replied, "Mr. President, I sent you a memorandum on those points."

FDR responded, "Leon, are you under the impression that I read those memoranda of yours? Why I can't even lift them!"

"He Knows When You've Been Bad or Good, So Be Good for Goodness Sake"

By 1935, FDR was riding high on his popularity with the working classes, but in the business community, his name was anathema.

Roosevelt knew this and was adept at playing the "class hatred" card. His fellow renegade patrician, Governor George Earle from Philadelphia, told him this story about the posh Rittenhouse Club in Philadelphia. FDR relished repeating the tale. It seems that some of the members were gathered around in the club's library grousing over "that man" while drinking their high-balls. Suddenly, they heard the familiar but hated voice coming out of the Atwater Kent radio in the club library: "There they sit in the well-warmed and well-stocked clubs. . . ."

One old member expostulated in fear, "Heavens, do you think that damned S.O.B. heard us?"

"Hold Your Hat"

Franklin Roosevelt was, along with Abraham Lincoln and Ronald Reagan, among the best presidential raconteurs. Like Lincoln, he brought to his storytelling ability the gifts of mimicry and timing. In telling of a senator who didn't know what he was talking about, Roosevelt related one of his favorite stories that concerned his preparatory school of Groton. The headmaster, who had presided over the school when Roosevelt attended, was Endicott Peabody. Peabody had invited the bishop of Boston to deliver a talk at an assembly on "sex." The prelate consented, but when his wife asked him what he was going to speak on, he replied, "Sailing." She shook her head in wonderment.

Some days later, the bishop's wife was on Newbury Street in Boston when she ran into a friend whose son was attending Groton.

"Oh," the friend said, "my son said your husband delivered such a wonderful talk at the school."

"Dear me, I don't know what he could have said," replied the bishop's wife. "The only time he ever tried it he lost his hat, got tangled in the sheets, and threw up."

Horse Sense?

When Franklin Roosevelt became president, he found himself burdened by files left by the previous administrators. Repeatedly, he called the State Department and asked if they could be removed to one of their storage sections. But the State Department gave him the runaround. They promised to get back to him but never did. Or they said there was no room for storage, when he knew there had to be.

One day he took matters into his own hands. He had himself wheeled to the old executive office building next door. With Undersecretary of State Sumner Welles accompanying him, he made an inspection at the close of the day's business.

At random, he picked an office halfway down the hall. FDR entered without announcement, to the consternation of State Department aides and clerks. Then he picked the middle drawer at random in the first filing cabinet he found. He opened a folder and read its title, "Horses in China."

"Horses in China, horsefeathers! I suppose this is an example of the top-priority files the State Department says cannot be destroyed. Well, they can now!"

"If at First You Don't Succeed . . ."

At a campaign rally in 1928 for governor, Roosevelt, while introducing a Democratic candidate for legislature who had previously lost the election, told this story of his days as assistant secretary of the navy. In his first years, they had to handle a backlog of complaints of naval retirees and their widows.

One widow wrote, "Mr. Secretary, my husband died eight years ago. I'm confined to bed with one doctor. I guess I'll try another."

"If It Ain't Broke, Don't Fix It."

In 1940 the president, while in New York speaking to a trade association, ran into an old acquaintance from the days when he headed a bonding firm in the twenties.

He asked his business friend how he was going to vote, expecting to hear him say something like, "I like you, but I can't go along with a third term."

On the circuit that year, FDR relished telling the business

executive's answer. "Well, I voted against you in 1932, but things got better. Then four years later I voted against you again, but still things picked up in our area. So why should I change my voting now and risking things going bad?"

In Deep "Do-Do"!

One of FDR's favorite stories to politicos to dramatize a big problem that could be mounting concerned his longtime playboy friend and fellow yachtsman George Earle. A Philadelphia blue blood whose ancestors came over with William Penn, he campaigned for Roosevelt in 1932 and then won the Pennsylvania governorship two years later, asking for a "little New Deal" in the Keystone State.

In the summer, the Pennsylvania chief executive opted to vacate the unair-conditioned executive mansion in Harrisburg for Pennsylvania's National Guard headquarters at a camp twenty miles southeast because of its privacy as well as its coolness— even though there were no inside plumbing facilities. When he wanted to signal a tryst with his current amour, he would hang his hat on the privy and she would repair to a designated spot in the woods nearby.

On one occasion, after affixing his hat to the door, he had to tend first to pressing business. The floor collapsed and the governor found himself not just metaphorically but literally into it up to his neck for twelve hours because he had given his state police bodyguard detail the Saturday off, and his current girlfriend got so tired of waiting in the woods that she got mad and left.

"It Takes One to Know One"

Both the business and political communities were shocked when President Franklin Roosevelt appointed Joseph Kennedy to head the newly created Securities and Exchange Commission. Roosevelt had gotten to know Kennedy during World War I, when Roosevelt was assistant secretary of the navy working on shipping contracts. Kennedy, who made himself a millionaire by the time he was in his thirties, did not always operate by Marquess of Queensberry Rules. He was known to have skirted on the illegal edge by piling up his fortune in commodity dealings.

When asked why he appointed Kennedy to clean up the stock market, FDR answered, "It takes a thief to catch a thief."

Knock-Kneed Kennedy

When Roosevelt had been reelected in 1936, he was pressed by Joseph Kennedy to appoint Kennedy ambassador to Britain.

The Irish Kennedy, who had long been snubbed by Boston patricians, coveted the top diplomat post for its social preeminence. FDR felt he had to accede to his wishes, since Kennedy had been a major contributor and, more important, a key player in rallying Irish Catholic voters to FDR's cause.

FDR invited Kennedy to dinner at the White House. After dinner, he told Kennedy he had to put on the knickers and stockings of the eighteenth-century costume in which a new ambassador must be clad in order to make his entrance in the Court of St. James's before the king. A disgruntled Kennedy at first refused but then agreed when the president insisted that it was necessary if he was to announce the appointment.

Kennedy donned the jacket, ruffled shirt, tight pants, and black slippers, and walked in front of the president. Roosevelt howled with laughter, to Kennedy's chagrin. "Joe," he pronounced, "I can't appoint you. We can't send out to London a bowlegged ambassador." Kennedy, who got the appointment, never forgave Roosevelt for the indignity.

Knockwurst Knockdown

In the early 1900s, Roosevelt, as a young man, was traveling through Germany. Next to him in the train car was an old friend of his mother. A Prussian officer entered their compartment and closed the window. The American woman, complaining of a headache, asked Roosevelt to open the window a bit, saying she needed the air. The Prussian captain slammed it shut. Roosevelt opened it again. When the officer rose to close it a third time, he was knocked to the floor by Franklin. When the train pulled into Berlin, the officer had Roosevelt arrested and taken to prison. The U.S. ambassador had Roosevelt released after his mother, Sara Delano Roosevelt, sent a cable to the embassy.

FDR relished telling the story to White House visitors in the thirties to illustrate the boorishness of the Germans. He would conclude that he took a swing at German militarism long before World War I and that he expected he would have to do it again.

Lah-Di-Dah!

As the menace of Hitler and Nazism reared its ugly head, Roosevelt sensed the need for America's own foreign intelligence-gathering. The president was overreliant on British intelligence. The FBI was limited to inside American shores. FDR asked New York attorney "Wild" Bill Donovan to form the Office of Strategic Services (OSS). Its critics, J. Edgar Hoover in particular, said it stood for "Oh So Social" because its recruits reflected FDR's background—Eastern prep schools and colleges such as Harvard, Yale, Princeton, and Williams.

The Mad Widow?

Roosevelt left Washington in 1921 to return to New York following his years as assistant secretary of the navy and then his losing campaign for vice president in 1920. Soon thereafter, he was offered the job as vice president of a bonding firm, U.S. Fidelity & Deposit Co. It was a mostly front-office ceremonial position that allowed Roosevelt time for his practice of law and politics.

One afternoon, an elegant lady clad in black and pearls came to his office. Angrily she told Roosevelt how U.S. F&D, working with the trustees of her husband's assets, had defrauded her and left her penniless.

Roosevelt, moved by her account, promised to assist her and get to the bottom of it. Not long after she left, the phone rang. A company executive asked, "Did that woman who just escaped from the state asylum stop in your office?"

Magic Moment

Harry Hopkins, FDR's close friend and top aide, was a widower who lived at the White House with his daughter, Diana. The visit of King George and Queen Elizabeth in June 1938 was a big moment in the seven-year-old's life. Shortly before the royal arrival, Diana lost a baby tooth and asked her father, when finding a quarter under her pillow, "What does the tooth fairy look like?"

"Like a fairy princess" was the answer.

Roosevelt heard all this and told Hopkins to bring his daughter up to the royal suite just before the state banquet for the king.

As Diana beheld Queen Elizabeth in a white gown with a diamond tiara in her hair, Roosevelt said to Diana, "That's what a fairy queen looks like and that tops a fairy princess any day."

"Mama Knows Best?"

The first visit by a British monarch to its former colonies was in 1938, and the first place the British king and queen stopped was Hyde Park on the Hudson, not the White House. The royal couple arrived in late afternoon on a train from Ottawa, Canada.

When Sara Delano Roosevelt saw her son with a shaker and cocktail glasses on the card table in the library, she took the shaker and gave a disdainful sniff at its contents of gin. "Now, Franklin, haven't you had enough of your little 'cocktails'? Surely after their long trip, the king and queen will want some tea."

When the king came downstairs, the president pointed to the martini shaker and glasses and said, "My mother thinks you would prefer tea."

George VI, the son of another straitlaced mother, Queen Mary, replied, "That's what my mother would say, too," as he reached for the martini glass.

Mama's Boy?

In early 1910, a delegation of Democratic politicians made their way from Albany, New York, to Hyde Park. Hyde Park was located in a heavily Republican district. They needed a sacrificial lamb in the state senate race.

Because of Theodore Roosevelt, who had left the White House the year before, the name of Roosevelt would add votes to the Democrat column.

Roosevelt listened carefully and then said, "I'd have to talk to my mother about it."

"Frank," replied the Democratic boss of the city of Albany, "there are men in Poughkeepsie waiting. They won't like to hear that you had to first ask your mama's permission."

Mixed Feelings?

Franklin Roosevelt, who considered himself the maestro mixologist in the making of cocktails, had one he called "my Haitian libation" that blended rum and gin together with pineapple juice. He usually served it to guests only on shipboard. On one occasion, his guest of honor was Winston Churchill, who had been taken on a little voyage by yacht down the Potomac. The prime minister, who much preferred Dewar's Scotch to drinks of an exotic sort, grimaced when the president, after rattling the ice-filled shaker, said, "And now, my masterpiece—the Haitian libation." The bibulous Churchill, who was never known to reject adult beverages, had this comment: "I have mixed feelings about mixed drinks."

Muchos Gracias, Mayor

As the Democratic National Convention in Chicago neared in 1932, Governor Franklin Roosevelt's chances of being nominated were good but by no means certain. Although he had the backing of the popular Mayor James Michael Curley in Boston, the Irish Democrats who remained loyal to former standard-bearer Al Smith had closed the door to any Roosevelt delegates. When Roosevelt contacted Curley, the mayor told the governor,

"I'm taking a vacation in Puerto Rico in the summer." Then he added, "But, Governor, don't worry. I'll be in Chicago to cast my vote."

When Puerto Rico was called, the first delegate to rise said, "I am Señor Jaime Miguel Curley, Mayor of Nuevo Boston, Puerto Rico"—he paused as the convention roared at the words of the colorful Boston politico—"and I cast my vote for Franklin Delano Roosevelt."

"A Multitude of Sins"

One morning during World War II, FDR woke and breakfasted in the upstairs residence. He was surprised to find Mrs. Roosevelt not around, unaware that she had left the White House at 6 A.M. to go with Maury Maverick of Texas to inspect a prison in Baltimore, Maryland. Maverick was head of an organization supervising work performed by convicts.

Not knowing this, FDR called his wife's secretary to inquire of her whereabouts. "Mr. President, your wife is in prison."

"You don't say. But, tell me, what crime did they finally nail her on?"

Murderer Made Marshal!

In matters of appointments, FDR, like all presidents, had to trade to get what he wanted. Senator "Cotton Ed" Smith from South Carolina was blocking the naming of Rex Tugwell as undersecretary of agriculture. The left-leaning Tugwell had been one of FDR's original "Brain Trust." Roosevelt won Smith's consent by making one of his South Carolina's political lieutenants a U.S. marshal, despite the fact that he had once been convicted of homicide.

"Rex," FDR said the next time they saw each other, "we got it for you, even though we had to make a murderer a marshal!"

"My Fellow Immigrants"

In April 1939, President Roosevelt, overriding advice from his advisers, kept his commitment to speak to the National Society of the Daughters of the American Revolution at the newly built Congress Hall, just one block below the White House. The reactionary organization, though nominally nonpolitical, had been quite outspoken against some proposed New Deal legislation.

The president opened his speech, "We are all sons and daughters of immigrants and revolutionaries."

"Name Your Poison"

In 1920 Franklin Roosevelt was the candidate for vice president with James Cox in the losing race against Warren Harding and Calvin Coolidge. The former assistant secretary of the navy in the Wilson administration traveled to more states and delivered more speeches than the other three candidates combined. His travels afforded him a fund of campaign stories, with which he later would regale his audiences with great relish when he was president.

In Kentucky, he told of meeting an old mountaineer at a rally in 1920 who did not understand the questions Roosevelt addressed to him. Zeke was his name, and he told Roosevelt that he was hard of hearing. He had gone to a doctor, who asked him how much mountain dew he was drinking a day. Zeke replied, "About a quart."

"Well," said the doctor, "at that rate, you are going to become completely deaf."

"What do you recommend?" asked Zeke.

"Well, if you want to keep your hearing, you'd better stop drinking."

Zeke replied, "If it's all the same to you, I like what I've been drinkin' better than what I've been hearin'. So I think I'll just become deef."

Native Customs?

As assistant secretary of the navy, the young, handsome, and socially prominent Roosevelt was a sought-after speaker with women's groups. But some of the same organizations harbored suspicions about American "imperialism" inflicted on the Pacific territories.

After one talk, an earnest young woman asked, "But, Mr. Roosevelt, do you think it's right to inflict our ways upon their native customs, thereby eliminating theirs?"

"Good question. In Samoa, there is the practice of 'famag'au,' in which fathers can auction off their daughters as young as nine or ten to men for the sole purpose of destroying the young girls' hymens—in other words, taking away their virginity. My good ladies, do you say we were wrong in stopping that?"

"Naughty Word"

FDR relished telling stories against himself. One favorite that later appeared in a magazine cartoon concerned graffiti written on a doorstep in Scarsdale, an upscale Westchester County suburban community that was rock-ribbed in its Republican loyalties.

A little girl was tattling to her mother on her younger brother.

"Lester has written a dirty word on the Johnstons' doorway." Expecting a word of the four-letter variety, instead the mother found emblazoned in black ink the nine-letter word ROOSEVELT.

"Nearer My God to Thee"

Franklin Roosevelt was a devout Episcopalian and regularly attended the small white St. John's Episcopal Church just opposite the White House next to Lafayette Park. In fact, the president became good friends with the St. John's rector, John Gillespie Magee, whose son volunteered for the Canadian Royal Air Force (RAF) in 1939.

Roosevelt relished reporting the story the rector told him. The Episcopalian priest answered the phone to hear an eager voice say, "Do you expect the president to be in church this Sunday? We'd love to be in the same room with him."

"I cannot promise," said the rector, "but as the president himself has said, 'a superior power or rather supreme power will be in attendance, and that should compel your presence.'"

Neither Friend nor Favor

In 1938 President Roosevelt was enduring a rough political

patch because of his attack on the Supreme Court and the declining employment numbers. His friend and top aide, Harry Hopkins, reported that one of his old friends had been saying some nasty things about him. Roosevelt said, "Is that so? When did this happen?"

Hopkins answered, "A few weeks ago."

FDR leaned back in his chair and took a puff from that long cigarette holder and opined," "That's strange. I don't recall ever doing him a favor."

Noah's Wine to Adam's Ale

As assistant secretary of the navy, Roosevelt often had to preside over the ceremonies for the launching of new ships at Norfolk, Virginia. On one occasion, a delegation from the Women's Temperance Society protested the use of alcohol to christen ships. "Wouldn't it be a salutary example for sobriety and temperance to break against the bow a bottle of grape juice instead?"

Roosevelt deftly dismissed the recommendation with this reply, "The long tradition of christening with champagne is already a splendid example of temperance. The ship takes its first sip of wine and then continues on water ever after."

"No 'Cain' Raising"

While in Warm Springs, Georgia, in 1925 for the recuperative waters, Roosevelt received an inquiry from a leg and arch support manufacturer whose letter was undermined by its illiteracy. The opening question was "Does Mr. Roosevelt use a 'cain'?"

FDR's answer was, "No, I do not use a CAIN because I am not ABEL."

"No Joking Matter"

Josephus Daniels, in World War I, was the secretary of the navy and Roosevelt's boss. A North Carolina Democrat, he had supported the presidential ambitions of William Jennings Bryan three times. At the 1912 Democratic Convention, Bryan, by shifting his support to Wilson, was named secretary of state. Daniels, for similar reasons, landed the navy position.

One day in the old executive building (the State, War, and Navy departments), Daniels was jesting with his assistant secretary. Poking Roosevelt in the ribs, Daniels pointed across to the White House and said, "Some day, Franklin, you'll be living there." He glanced at Roosevelt, who did not find the prediction amusing. Daniels was only stating what Roosevelt regarded as fact.

No Portrait of a Cap[e]on!

The intimate friendship between Franklin Roosevelt and the comely New York socialite Lucy Mercer dated back to World War I when Miss Mercer acted as a social secretary for Assistant Secretary of the Navy Roosevelt. At one point, according to some reports, Roosevelt even considered marrying Lucy and taking up a career in the navy. Eleanor Roosevelt found love letters from Lucy, and the marriage almost dissolved. But Roosevelt ended the affair, and the Roosevelt marriage became a cold political partnership.

Lucy Mercer married Winthrop Rutherford of New Jersey. When he died, the president would occasionally secretly meet Lucy. In April 1945, FDR's daughter arranged, without her mother's knowledge, a meeting at Warm Springs, Georgia. Lucy Rutherford brought with her Elizabeth Shoumatoff, the Russian artist who had painted a portrait of the president a year earlier. The artist was painting the president clad in a navy-blue cape. The working title by the Russian artist was "The President and Cape On."

"No, no," said Mercer, "it should be 'President Wearing a Cape'—he is no cap[e]on!"

FDR laughed.

No Rush Job

In early 1945, President Roosevelt wrote Prime Minister Churchill about the agenda for the six-day conference of "the Big Powers" at Yalta. FDR felt there was no reason that the plan for creating the United Nations could not be completed in the conference session. Churchill was doubtful. "I don't see any way of realizing our hopes for a world organization in six days. Even the Almighty took seven."

No Spittin' Image?

Governor Roosevelt, in showing around visitors in the executive mansion in Albany, New York, would point to the many brass spittoons and regale his visitors with this story.

Shortly after he was inaugurated in January 1929, his mother, Sara Delano Roosevelt, had motored over from Hyde Park to visit with her son. One afternoon she invited some of her old Albany friends to tea in the mansion.

One of the friends offered this comment, "There are a lot of spittoons here, aren't there, Sara?"

"Yes," Mrs. Roosevelt replied, "but the great thing is that in all his eight years of being here, Governor Smith never missed."

"Not One of the Four Hundred"

Sara Delano Roosevelt was more than just the legal owner of Hyde Park—the Roosevelt manor house on the Hudson—she knew intimately the history of every chair, table, highboy, and armoire, as well as each piece of china, whether it was a wedding gift or passed down from her Delano side or the Roosevelt's.

It was her house, and visitors in this house were her guests. At one luncheon, she looked over to her right and saw her son Franklin turning to talk to a man on his right—a visitor in garish yellow suspenders, no coat or tie on, a garish purple striped shirt—who was employing earthy language unsuitable for table conversation. She turned to Eleanor, her daughter-in-law, on her left, and said in a loud stage whisper, "Who is that dreadful little man in my house talking to Franklin?" She was told it was Senator Huey Long of Louisiana, whom the president had invited to discuss some legislation.

"Oh, What a Tangled Web We Weave . . ."

When Roosevelt was assistant secretary of the navy in World War I, a navy clerk, who had the key to FDR's office for maintenance purposes, one night, to help idle the time away, ran across a form recommending the Congressional Medal of Honor. He filled in his name, concocted some cock-and-bull story of heroism, signed Roosevelt's name, and sent a copy of it to his wife as a lark. His wife was so impressed that she called the newspapers before her husband could tell her it was a joke.

Roosevelt called him on the carpet and read a form that filed charges of "forgery, fraud, impersonation, and violation of the U.S. mail" against the stricken seaman first class. FDR then tore up the form. "It wouldn't be fair," he said later. "I had such a good time dining out on that story afterward."

"Old Bastard"

When France surrendered to Germany in June 1940, Britain stood alone against Hitler. On the second floor of the White House, the president, with his friend and top aide Harry Hopkins, listened on the radio to Prime Minister Winston Churchill's impassioned address to the British people and the Commonwealth natives. The concluding peroration carried these words: "We shall fight them on the beaches, we shall fight them on the landing grounds, we shall fight them on the streets and in the hills." And then with a steely tone in his voice, "We shall never surrender."

After the speech, FDR turned to Hopkins and said, "As long

as that old bastard's around, Britain will never surrender. It's not money down the rat hole, as in the case of France!"

Old Curiosity Shop?

The reading of Charles Dickens's *A Christmas Carol* was always the centerpiece of holiday activities at Hyde Park. Roosevelt would sit in his favorite high-backed chair next to the fireplace in the living room and read aloud the Dickens classic to his family with all the newest grandchildren present. He would assume the various voices of the characters—Scrooge, the ghosts, Bob Cratchit, Tiny Tim, and all.

On what would be his last Christmas in 1944, Roosevelt found he had competition for center stage, and it was not from Hollywood actress Faye Emerson who had recently married his son Elliott. It was from little James, three years old, who had noted something odd about his grandfather's mouth. He crawled up in the midst of Roosevelt's reading and announced, "Grandpa, you have a tooth missing!" Roosevelt tried to keep reading, but the boy said, "It's right there," pointing with his finger to the lower left side of the president's mouth. "Did you swallow it?"

FDR closed the book, in a paroxysm of laughter, saying, "There's too much competition in this house."

A Pachyderm's Position?

In the 1940 campaign, FDR lampooned the Republican Party for the inconsistency of its positions—its presidential candidate stretched out for intervention while its platform curled back into isolation. Its leading spokesmen on trade matters took stands both high and low on tariffs.

"If the old elephant of the GOP can contort itself into all these positions at the same time, it would be a Ringling Brothers' prize attraction."

Petticoat Power

Just after his victory in 1940 to an unprecedented third term, Roosevelt held a press conference. In his winning campaign, FDR had lashed out at the special interests and lobbies lined up behind his opponent. A reporter asked the question, "Mr. President, I suppose you will consult the powerful interests that control you before making your cabinet selections."

"Young man," Roosevelt snapped back in mock protest, "I would ask that you keep my wife's name out of it."

Plain Speaking

When World War II began, blackouts were enforced in every

city because of fear of bombings by Germany on the East Coast or by Japan on the West. The head of the Government Services Administration (GSA) presented to Roosevelt in the Oval Office a placard to be posted in every government and post office building across the nation.

With pride the bureaucrat intoned the words on the poster card: "It is obligatory that all illumination be extinguished before the premises are vacated."

Roosevelt answered, "Why the hell can't you say, 'Put out the lights when you leave'?"

"Play It Again..."

On New Year's Eve 1941, President Roosevelt hosted a small intimate dinner at the White House for his top aide and a few friends. After dinner, before champagne toasts at the midnight hour for the new year, the movie *Casablanca*, starring Ingrid Bergman and Humphrey Bogart was played for the guests.

The movie selection was an inside joke between the president and Harry Hopkins. The day before, Roosevelt had set up a second meeting with Prime Minister Churchill for January in Casablanca, Morocco.

"Po' Little Rich Girl"

When the United States entered World War I in 1917, President Wilson established tight controls over the use of energy and the purchase of foodstuffs during this wartime emergency. Wilson even used the White House lawn for the grazing of sheep as an example of economy.

A reporter from the *Washington Times* came out to interview the wife of FDR (at the time he was the assistant secretary of the navy). After Eleanor had left Washington for Campobello, the story appeared in the newspaper. Her irate husband, protective of his political future, sarcastically wired his wife. "Babs—Congratulations—you've made us a fortune on a future book—*How Millionaires Can Save Money.*" In the article, Eleanor had explained how she had halved her staff from twenty to ten, sold one of their three cars, and that they were now eating fish two nights a week instead of meat every night, as well as other savings, such as turning off the electric lights fifteen minutes earlier every night.

Mrs. Roosevelt was devastated by the story and by her husband's reaction.

Poppycock!

FDR, as president, did more for struggling artists and the arts than any previous chief executive. Yet his interest in the visual arts was limited. It began with the Hudson River School and ended with Winslow Homer's seascapes. Modern art, particularly of the abstract variety, received very little of his esteem.

Once, reportedly, he was shown a large abstract whose unencumbered beige background was punctuated in the center with a big brownish dot. To the shock of admiring matrons, Roosevelt gave his comment, "Poppycock!" Then he explained that was the old Dutch word for poultry excrement. "And I expect," he added, "that is the source for the tincture of that dot in the center."

Porcellian Pariah

FDR more than once said that the greatest disappointment in his life was the rejection of his membership in the Porcellian Club, Harvard's most elite private club, to which his father had belonged. The pain of that turndown he never felt more keenly than at the White House in 1908.

Alice, his wife's cousin and the daughter of President Theodore Roosevelt, was marrying Nicholas Longworth, a Republican congressman from Cincinnati, Ohio. The White House wedding was the biggest social event in many a year. Eleanor Roosevelt was at that time pregnant with her first child, Anna, and because she always felt dowdy in comparison to her chic and glamorous cousin Alice, she sent her regrets. But Franklin would not miss the chance to be part of this gala event.

But a Porcellian meeting upstairs at the White House before the wedding plunged him into despair. Since Longworth and some of his ushers were members, President Theodore Roosevelt, who was a member of Harvard's most prestigious club, had called for a private meeting of Porcellians upstairs at the White House. He even had the way paved for Walter, the black custodian of the Porcellian Club in Cambridge, to be the steward for the private club's ceremonies. Then at the reception, Franklin had to experience the humiliation of the president calling out "Brother" Longworth and the other Harvard Porcellian attendees as "Brothers," but Franklin was not among the "Brothers."

Potted?

When Roosevelt was governor of New York, he enjoyed presiding over the daily cocktail hour in his Albany office. Judge Sam Rosenman, who was the governor's principal legal adviser as well as his main speechwriter, regarded his attendance at these sessions at the end of the day as obligatory. Rosenman, however, was not an imbiber. So he'd dutifully nurse a Manhattan, but as soon as the governor would sight Rosenman's almost empty glass, Roosevelt would say, "Another little sippy?" Now, Rosenman had difficulty in finishing his first drink. When confronted with the second drink, he would look for the nearest potted plant and then dump the contents when no one was looking. One day, Roosevelt announced to his cocktail audience, "We've noticed some of the potted plants' leaves have turned into some weird colors—so we had the state Department of Agriculture examine the plants in their labs. Their scientific analysis reports the soil has been contaminated with alcohol. We are bewildered at how this soil has been so polluted."

Rosenman owned up and said, "If you want to keep your plants healthy, you better pass up on giving me seconds."

Presidential Pardon

For the White House Correspondents Dinner in March 1944, the ailing president rallied to display his usual witty good form. In a mock takeoff on his much-imitated "I hate war" remarks, FDR roared, "I love humanity; Eleanor loves humanity; Fala loves humanity; we all love humanity. . . .

"And in that spirit and magnanimity, I shall exercise my presidential authority and grant a pardon to those of you sentenced to attend tomorrow's press conference."

Presidents Come and Go

The author of *The Education of Henry Adams* was living across from the White House during World War I. Henry Adams remembered well from his boyhood his grandfather, John Quincy Adams, whose father, John Adams, had also occupied the executive mansion. Though much older, Henry Adams was a close friend of Theodore Roosevelt, Franklin's cousin. Adams had also authored the first American political novel, *Democracy*, that cynically skewered Washington life.

The lugubrious Adams encountered the assistant secretary of the navy one day in Lafayette Park.

"Young man, I have lived in this house many years and have seen the occupants of the White House across the square come and go, and nothing you minor officials or occupants of that house do will affect the history of this world for long."

Putting on the Dog?

For Sara Delano Roosevelt, the matriarch of the family in the Hyde Park manor on the Hudson River, the visit of King George VI and his queen to the Roosevelt house was the most momentous occasion in the history of the Roosevelt family. Sara Delano Roosevelt had grown up in the latter half of the nineteenth century, when

Queen Victoria was an icon. Now her son had decided to host the great-grandson of Victoria with a picnic outside instead of a formal luncheon at the house. "Franklin, you mean you are going to give the king and queen wieners for their meal?"

"Mama, he's going to love an American hot dog in a bun with all the fixings."

And the king did!

Rearview Mirror

Franklin Roosevelt cherished his Harvard years, when he was editor of the Harvard *Crimson*. Later, he felt honored when he was chosen grand marshal of the procession of his twenty-fifth class reunion in 1929. He was then governor of New York. Eight years later, as president, he read reports from one old classmate, who had told a reporter the president was the most unpopular member of his class.

"'Old Binkie,' was it?" asked FDR. "He was a reactionary when he was young, too."

"Rowed on the crew, did he?" asked his fellow Harvard man and Undersecretary of State Sumner Welles.

"Oh, yes," said FDR, "quite good—one of those who thought you only moved forward while looking backward."

A Red-Faced Roosevelt

In 1940, when Britain stood alone against the Hitler menace, Prime Minister Churchill sent a new ambassador to the United States, Lord Lothian. Although the United States was officially neutral, Roosevelt informally would send signals that America supported Britain in its fight for survival. One of these symbolic moves was his invitation to Lothian to have dinner with him in the private upstairs residence of the White House.

After dinner, Roosevelt, wanting to emphasize the historic bonds tying together the two greatest English-speaking nations, said: "Lothian, American presidents dating back to Lincoln have always taken extra steps to accommodate the British ambassador. Why in 1863, the British ambassador found himself stranded by a Civil War curfew behind the locked gates of Lafayette Park opposite the White House with the wife of the Spanish envoy."

Distressed by this lockout with his girlfriend in this tryst, he sighted a friend walking down Pennsylvania Avenue. It was Secretary of State William Seward.

"Seward, Seward. You must get a key to unlock me."

Seward replied, "No problem. I'll get [Edwin] Stanton [secretary of war]. He has a key."

"No, no," answered the British diplomat. "He's a 'shouting Methodist' and will give me a sermon about my morals."

"Never mind," responded Seward. "I'll go to the president. He has a key."

But Lincoln, although eager to help, found his disorganized office unequal to the challenge. The key could not be found. But Lincoln had a solution. A stepladder was in the basement. The two men—president and secretary of state—hauled the twelve-foot ladder across Pennsylvania Avenue, and the ambassador and his inamorata climbed over the gate.

Concluded FDR, "You see, Lothian, American presidents have always tried to come to rescue British diplomats in time of trouble."

The lack of response from Lothian, who was looking fixedly at the ceiling, left the president nonplussed.

"But American presidents always are ready to assist their English cousins," reasserted FDR.

"Mr. President," replied Lothian, "the diplomat you speak of was my grandfather."

Republican Refusal

Roosevelt was not averse to regaling audiences at the White

House with stories in which he was the butt of the joke. He relished telling this tale.

"In Guadalcanal, our marines at a machine-gun pillbox faced a charge of Japanese who were shouting, 'To hell with Roosevelt!' When the corporal did not unleash his weapon upon the foe, his sergeant said, 'Corporal, why aren't you opening fire?' The corporal explained, as Roosevelt applied the punch line, 'I can't bring myself to shoot fellow Republicans.'"

Right Bite

In August 1943, President Roosevelt met Prime Minister Churchill in Quebec for wartime planning. Their host was Canadian Prime Minister Mackenzie King. The bachelor premier lived with his mother, and among his eccentricities, he was a spiritualist who communicated with the dead. Roosevelt, as well as Churchill, did not especially want to hear Wellington or Nelson's views on the war, and they were annoyed when King inserted himself into the strategy sessions.

Afterward, Prime Minister Churchill and Minister King were invited down to Hyde Park, Roosevelt's home on the Hudson. One member of the Roosevelt family did not offer a kind welcome. It was Rex, Mrs. Roosevelt's German shepherd, who bit King on the ankle.

The president reportedly laughed when he was told of the unfortunate news.

"Better his ankle than his ass, because that's where he does most of his thinking."

Right On?

"Hundred Days" is the phrase that would describe the frantic pace of executive action in the first three and half months of the New Deal. (Brain truster Raymond Moley would try to correct it precisely to one hundred five days.)

In 1937 a small hit musical, *I'd Rather Be Right*, played on Broadway. It attempted to describe in music and words those "Hundred Days." George M. Cohan (who would later be known as "Yankee Doodle Dandy" because of the movie of that name in which Jimmy Cagney would have the title role) would play Roosevelt. One hit song from the musical *I'd Rather Be Right* was "Take a Law, Mac." Ross McIntyre had actually been the appointments secretary, but FDR, in calling in Grace Tully for dictation, would say in words where fact followed fiction:

"Take a law, Grace."

Roosevelt Retreat

Shortly after Pearl Harbor, President Roosevelt invited Prime Minister Churchill to be his guest at the White House. In a busy week, the two heads of the Allied governments met daily to discuss strategy.

One late morning, Roosevelt thought of something he had to ask Churchill. He, in his wheelchair, propelled himself over to the Monroe Room at the White House. There to his astonishment he found the prime minister in the "altogether"—pink-fleshed from emerging from his morning bath. Roosevelt wheeled around and beat his retreat, despite a plea from Churchill. "The king's first minister has nothing to hide from the president of the United States."

"The Russians Are Coming"

The Communist revolution in 1917, led by Lenin, massacred the czar and his family and then overthrew the democratic parliament of Prime Minister Alexander Kerensky. Since that time, the presidential administrations of Wilson, Harding, Coolidge, and Hoover had all refused to recognize the new Soviet Union. But in 1933 President Roosevelt opened diplomatic relations with the Kremlin.

Most of the foreign policy establishment was shocked. Yet few were more upset than the president's own mother, who thought the assassinations, wholesale killings, and mass purges were the work of savages, not of a civilized government.

"Franklin," she said, "You've seen the last of me in the White House. I'll never go there again."

She was back in four weeks, however, to visit her son.

"Same Old, Same Old"

At a White House dinner in early December 1940, six weeks before his third inauguration, FDR found himself talking to Chief Justice Charles Evans Hughes, who would administer the oath of office.

"Mr. President," said Hughes, "how about if just after you are sworn in, I lean forward and whisper, 'Don't you think this is getting a little monotonous for both of us?'"

Security Pants?

While Roosevelt was shaving in the upstairs residence bathroom at the White House, he thought of something that his new young press secretary, Bill Hassett, should be briefed on. He sent his valet down to get him.

When Hassett entered, FDR told him, "Sit on the can, Bill, but remember while you are on the throne, the seat is up."

"The Sheik of Araby"

On Valentine's Day 1945, Roosevelt was on the U.S. destroyer *Hudson* docking in Cairo. The president's entourage had left the Yalta meeting and was stopping in Egypt on the way back to America. The president called in his twenty-five-year-old daughter Anna, nicknamed "Sissy," while he was breakfasting just before a scheduled visit of the Saudi feudal head.

"Sis," he said, "here's one hundred dollars. Go into Cairo and buy all the pretties you want. Either that or you can stay locked in your stateroom."

"But I want to stay and meet the king of Saudi Arabia."

"No. Ibn Saud is a strict Muslim. He has plenty of wives. However, the true Muslim will not permit women in his company with other men. A woman in such a situation is for sex, Sis, so when he sees a woman he confiscates her."

Then FDR spooned some cream and peaches in his mouth—"like a peach sundae."

Signature Piece

Sara Delano Roosevelt, the Hyde Park dowager, and Louis Howe, the seedy Albany politico, were from different worlds. They had only one mutual interest—Franklin Roosevelt, the up-and-coming New York state senator. Mrs. Roosevelt disdained the disheveled, chain-smoking Howe, who occupied so much of her son's time. In 1910 Howe set up a meeting for Franklin and Governor Woodrow Wilson in his Trenton capitol office. The reform New Jersey governor was a good bet for his party's presidential nomination in 1912.

Roosevelt, a like-minded Democratic reformer, campaigned hard for the Wilson presidential candidacy, which triumphed. Then Roosevelt eagerly pursued the job of assistant secretary of the navy, a job that his cousin Theodore had used as a launching pad.

Not even Roosevelt was happier than Howe when his boss secured the job. For the first time as Roosevelt's assistant, Howe knew he would have a steady income.

"What will you do for Franklin?" the mother asked Howe.

"I can forge his signature the way you like it—big. You always said, Mrs. Roosevelt—'a great man has a great signature.'"

Sleepless on the Second Floor?

At one of the "speech-writing" working sessions in the White House in 1942 that consisted of Harry Hopkins and Robert Sherwood, Roosevelt wanted to have inserted, "Sometimes I can't sleep at night worrying about your sons overseas."

Hopkins, lifting his eyes to the ceiling, said, "Come on, Mr. President, historians will be reading your speeches. They will learn you never had a sleepless night in your life. Once you hit the pillow at ten o'clock, you sleep soundly for eight hours!"

Solomonic Solution

In 1942 President Roosevelt journeyed to Morocco to parley with Prime Minister Winston Churchill. The discussions centered on the battle in North Africa where the newly combined American and British commands were fighting Rommel's Afrika Korps. The difficulty in fusing together the two nations' armies was symbolized by the difference in the dining traditions in the top officers' mess. Specifically, the Americans liked cocktails or highballs before dinner but didn't imbibe while eating. The Brits liked their wine during dinner but didn't raise their glass until the ranking general called for a toast to the king.

Churchill suggested to FDR a melding of the best in both

traditions. "Drinks before dinner, during dinner, and for that matter, after dinner."

"A solution worthy of Solomon," said FDR.

A Spanking Good Idea!

In 1928 Governor Al Smith of New York was nominated to be the Democratic candidate for president. If he did not carry his own state—the state with the most electoral votes—he had no hope of winning the presidency. He needed a strong candidate to run to succeed him as governor, which would buttress the Democratic vote.

The crippled Franklin Roosevelt had a popular name. Smith had friends sound out Roosevelt, but both FDR's adviser Louis Howe and his wife, Eleanor, were opposed. Roosevelt gave health as his reason for saying no. Smith said, "You don't have to be an acrobat to be governor."

Again and again, Smith called FDR, to no avail. Then FDR's daughter, Anna, sent him a telegram:

"GO AHEAD AND TAKE IT."

Roosevelt took her advice and called Smith. Then he wired Anna:

"YOU OUGHT TO BE SPANKED. MUCH LOVE. PA.

Square Root

Harry Hopkins, FDR's closest adviser and political friend, was not a prepossessing figure. Untidy in clothes, disheveled in appearance, and slight in frame, he would be lost in a crowd—looking like a nerdish clerk or bookkeeper uninterested in sports or parties.

But behind that superficial appearance, Hopkins possessed a unique talent for stripping problems to their essential question, with a disdain for euphemisms or distractions.

Once, when Churchill was laughing with FDR in the White House, supposedly to hash out problems for a joint press conference that afternoon, the two leaders were refighting the naval battles of Nelson and John Paul Jones. It took Hopkins to bring the principals down to business and address the problem at hand.

When Hopkins did so, Churchill, with his usual bluntness, said, "Harry, when this war is over, His Majesty's government is going to confer on you a noble title."

Hopkins sourly replied, "Membership in the House of Lords is one reward I don't covet."

"But Harry," continued Churchill, "we have already selected the title. You are to be named 'Lord Root of the Matter.'"

Steely Response?

By the time of the inauguration in 1933, the one-time friendship between Herbert Hoover and Franklin Roosevelt had soured into enmity. The traditional ride from the White House to the Capitol for the swearing in was not punctuated with the usual forced amenities and banalities. A glum Hoover stared out the window away from his successor. Roosevelt waited for Hoover to say something. The limousine passed the Commerce Department building, which was still under construction. It had been started in 1928, when Hoover was secretary of commerce. Standing the silence no longer, Roosevelt pointed and said, "Lovely steel." Hoover managed only a low grunt. Those were the only words spoken during the ride.

Succinct Summary

When President Franklin D. Roosevelt was a young lawyer starting out in New York before World War I, he was retained to handle a difficult civil case. The opposing lawyer was a polished practitioner of the bar and an eloquent advocate who completely outshone his young adversary in his argument to the jury. The veteran attorney's mastery, however, led to one mistake. Proud of his silver oratory, he spoke too long. Roosevelt noted the jury's wandering attention in the lawyer's summation.

Roosevelt rose, playing a hunch, and said, "Gentlemen, you have heard the evidence. You have also listened to my distinguished colleague, a brilliant orator. If you believe him and disbelieve the evidence, you will have to decide in his favor. That's all I have to say."

The jury was out only five minutes and brought in a verdict for Roosevelt's client.

Taking Liberties?

Francis Biddle, Roosevelt's attorney general, was a Philadelphia Biddle whose Quaker lineage was as impeccable as his decorum, and his precise mustache as trimmed as his humor. Punctilious in legal matters, his literal approach made him a pawn for FDR's inclination to tease.

One day, just before the attorney general was to come into FDR's office, FDR said to two of his aides, "Boys, don't give me away. Francis is keen on civil liberties and its erosion during a war, and I'm going to spin a line to him."

"Francis, I'm glad you came. We've been discussing civil liberties and the dangers it opens up, and I'm going to ask you to draft an order abrogating, as much as possible, all freedom of information. It's a tough thing, but I'm convinced it's absolutely necessary. . . ." Biddle looked thunderstruck and then launched an impassioned argument against it for five minutes until FDR and the others broke out laughing. At that point, Biddle realized his leg was being pulled.

Tale of the West

In 1940 when Hitler's armies swallowed up the continent of Europe, Congress forced through the Neutrality Act that forbade President Roosevelt from assisting Britain in their war against Nazi Germany. But Roosevelt, invoking the Monroe Doctrine, had written in a big exception. The Western Hemisphere had to be kept free of German meddling. Argentina and other South American countries at that time hosted many Fascist followers.

When Germany took over Denmark, its Iceland colony in the North Atlantic was threatened. Roosevelt had a map specifically made to show Iceland was in the Western Hemisphere. He displayed the counterfeit chart in the Map Room at the White House to his naval chief of staff and, accordingly, the American navy established a base in Reykjavík, Iceland. Roosevelt had spun a fast one over the U.S. Navy and Congress.

Norse-speaking Iceland is as much a part of Europe as Norway and Denmark. Yet it could be argued that Roosevelt was in a sense as right geographically as he was pragmatically. Underneath the small island of Iceland, the two tectonic plates—the North American shield and the European shield—sit about twenty feet from each other.

Teddy's Toddy

Franklin Roosevelt had just settled in as assistant secretary of the navy in the new Woodrow Wilson administration in 1913 when he received an SOS call from his most famous predecessor in his naval post—his distant cousin and uncle by marriage, Theodore Roosevelt. The former president's attempt to return to the White House had been sunk in his defeat by Governor Wilson. In the campaign, the bully bonhomie of Teddy was attributed to drunkenness by a Michigan newspaper editor. Roosevelt promptly initiated a libel suit.

When the case came to trial in May, the assistant secretary of the navy left Washington to be a character witness for his cousin, stating that not only did he never see his famous relative drunk but he never witnessed him ever drinking more than one glass of wine. The former president (unlike his younger cousin) testified he "never drank a cocktail or highball in his life."

JAMES C. HUMES

The defense lawyer countered with reports that he swilled mint juleps at the White House. Teddy admitted that the White House steward occasionally gave him a mint julep (which was made with Canadian rye, not Kentucky bourbon) as a sleeping sedative.

Notwithstanding his julep-sipping, Teddy won his suit, partly due to his Democratic cousin's testimony. The former president, however, waived the awarding of damages.

"There Goes the Neighborhood"

In 1943 FDR hosted Prime Minister Winston Churchill for the first time at his Hyde Park residence. As the squire of this old manor estate on the Hudson River, Roosevelt proudly told his British visitor, "My Roosevelt ancestors were the first here, and we've been here for seven generations."

Churchill, whose grandmother on the American Jerome side, was one-quarter Iroquois Indian, replied, "And my ancestors, Mr. President, were the first to greet them when your ancestors arrived."

A Thinking Man's President

Roosevelt never agonized or lost sleep over decisions. His style was more instinctive than intellectual.

The political writer John Gunther, in a piece on the president, once interviewed FDR's wife, Eleanor.

"Mrs. Roosevelt, how does the president think?" he asked.

"My dear Mr. Gunther, the president never thinks! He decides!"

Third-Rater?

In late March 1933, the newly inaugurated President Roosevelt paid a call on Justice Oliver Wendell Holmes. The newly retired nonagenarian lived right across from the White House, next to Lafayette Park.

Tommy "the Cork" Corcoran, a former clerk to the justice, now a lawyer writing some of the first-hundred-days legislation, was with Holmes when the president arrived. He went into a closet to listen in on the meeting.

Roosevelt boomed, "Mr. Justice, what are you doing this beautiful spring morning?"

"Reading Greek, Mr. President" came the reply.

"Why would anyone be reading Greek?" the president asked.

"To improve my mind, Mr. President."

"Mr. Justice"—Roosevelt's tone turned serious—"you have

lived more than half of the history of this great republic. What advice can you give me?"

"Mr. President, we are in a warlike crisis. You must marshal the battalions and fight," stated Holmes, referring to the Depression.

When the president left, Corcoran asked the justice, "What do you think of him?"

Holmes answered, "He is like his cousin Theodore—first-class temperament, third-rate mind."

"This Little Piggy Went to Market"

Endicott Peabody was the legendary founder and headmaster of Groton, the elite New England boarding school that FDR attended in his youth. The Episcopalian cleric was a dominating and much-admired figure in Roosevelt's formative years. Peabody was proud of all his Grotonians, but his two favorite grads, whose achievements he most boasted about as exemplifying civic duty, were Franklin Roosevelt, president of the United States, and Richard Whitney, president of the New York Stock Exchange. Both, after graduating from Groton, went to Harvard, where Whitney gained membership in the Porcellian Club (FDR's greatest regret was his failure to become a Porcellian).

In 1935 Whitney was sent to Sing Sing prison in Ossining, New York, for fraud and misappropriation of funds. A photo of Whitney showed him handcuffed to a fellow prisoner—a rapist. Whitney, however, was his ever-dapper self, wearing the gold figure of the Porcellian pig on a chain across his vest.

When he was shown the picture, FDR said, "Poor Dickie got piggy."

"Thunder over China"

Three Roosevelt women made the Hyde Park manor house on the Hudson their home—Eleanor, wife of the president; Betty, widow of James, FDR's older half-brother; and Sara Delano Roosevelt, the owner of Hyde Park and mother of the president.

When King George and Queen Elizabeth visited in June 1938, the resources of all three women were marshaled to meet the huge entertaining needs for the big party. Roosevelt, over his mother's objections, insisted on an American picnic, but the idea of paper plates for the residents of Buckingham Palace was preposterous. "Why, I never heard of such a thing . . ." began Sara Delano Roosevelt's vociferous veto of such a notion.

The Delano china that came from the family shipping trade

was not enough. Betty Roosevelt's china had to be borrowed. James Roosevelt, the president's older half-brother, and his second wife, Betty, had been married in London when he was an aide with the U.S. embassy. Betty was a live-wire Cockney who dropped her "aitches" like Eliza Doolittle in *My Fair Lady*, but she had inherited dinner sets from her husband's first wife, an Astor who had died. If Sara had her problems with the bawdy Betty, the Astor Spodeware she had was exquisite.

During the picnic outside, a huge crash was heard in the manor kitchen.

Betty took Sara's hand and imparted, "I 'ope, dearie, it's not my china that 'as just been broken."

"A Tisket, a (C)asket, a Yellow-Ribboned Basket ..."

During World War I, the Roosevelt family would avoid the steamy summer of Washington, D.C., by packing up and going off to Campobello, leaving Daddy behind. Shortly after their arrival on the Canadian island, Eleanor Roosevelt received a telegram from her husband: "WHAT SHOULD I DO WITH THE CASKET? FRANKLIN."

It seems in the hurry to pack their belongings before the taxi arrived to take them to the train station, they had left behind a basket. Because of a telegrapher's typo, the item changed form.

It became an often-told family joke.

Underground Money

The chances looked good for FDR's reelection in 1936, though campaign contributions would be needed against the big money that business interests would throw in to defeat the New Deal. John L. Lewis, the head of the coal miners' union, had endured Hoover in 1932 and had his share of run-ins with FDR. Now he wanted to come to the White House and publicly endorse the president in a photo op.

At the White House in the Oval Office with photographers poised, an ebullient Lewis said, "Mr. President, the coal miners enthusiastically support you, and here is their check for two hundred fifty thousand dollars."

The cagey president had sensed such a trap and replied, "John, take it back. We'll call you if we need you."

There was no picture, but FDR's aides did call Lewis from time to time for contributions.

Up Front!

In 1912 Democrat Woodrow Wilson won the presidency because

former President Theodore Roosevelt, with his "Bull Moose" Progressive Party, split the Republicans and President Taft lost. Elihu Root, secretary of war under McKinley, had managed the Taft forces at the GOP convention to beat back Theodore Roosevelt.

Josephus Daniels was named by President-elect Wilson to be secretary of the navy, and Franklin Roosevelt was lobbying hard to get the number-two job of the navy, just as cousin Theodore had been assistant secretary in the first term of President McKinley when Root was secretary of war.

Daniels told Root he was considering Franklin Roosevelt as assistant secretary.

"Watch out," replied Root. "He's a Roosevelt. When they ask someone to give them a ride, they mean to sit in the driver's seat."

Vice Precedence?

As the Democratic National Convention neared, the question of vice presidential running mate for an ailing and increasingly frail President Roosevelt took on crucial importance. Organized labor demanded the renomination of the incumbent vice president, Henry Wallace. Wallace was also the particular political darling of Eleanor Roosevelt. For much of the rest of the Democratic Party, the idea of the quixotic and leftist Wallace as president was scary. The Democratic National Committee chairman, Robert Hannegan of Missouri, relayed these concerns to FDR. Acceding to pressure, the president wrote a letter to Hannegan that offered the names of the leftist Justice William O. Douglas and the moderate Senator Harry S. Truman as vice presidential candidates.

Hannegan, saying that the letter had become blotted, went back to the president's secretary to have a new copy typed up. But in reading the text, he put the name of fellow Missourian Truman before the more leftist Justice Douglas. It would have historic consequences.

"Victory at Sea"

In 1914 Assistant Secretary of the Navy Roosevelt was invited to a banquet by Secretary of State William Jennings Bryan. The dinner was honoring the Japanese ambassadors and admirals for the tenth anniversary of the victory over the Russian navy in the Russo-Japanese War. (For peaceful settlement of the war, Roosevelt's cousin President Theodore Roosevelt had won the Nobel Peace Prize.)

Franklin Roosevelt noticed that the Japanese were miffed that the teetotaling, fundamentalist Baptist Bryan had no cham-

pagne at the head table. Roosevelt was embarrassed for the
United States that its top diplomat would allow this affront to the
Japanese honor. He reportedly slipped a note to a Bryan aide.

Bryan rose and said, "I toast in water because the great impe-
rial navy of Japan won their victory on water. When their navy
wins a victory on wine, I will toast them in wine."

The Japanese faces beamed.

Walk in the Park?

In 1917 Assistant Secretary of the Navy Franklin Roosevelt was as-
signed one day to escort British Foreign Secretary Lord Balfour,
who was visiting Washington for talks on the Allied cooperation
in World War I. (Today his name is remembered through the
Balfour Declaration promising a Jewish state earlier that year.)

Roosevelt took the cricket-loving Balfour to watch a baseball
game. The hometown Washington Senators were playing the
New York Yankees. As Roosevelt explained the game, Balfour
tried to follow. "Instead of two wickets," Balfour said in explana-
tion to himself, "there are four bases and the batsman, who, like
in cricket, hits the ball, trying to run to the first base."

"Yes," replied Roosevelt. "You've got the hang of it."

Just then a Yankee batter at bat received four wide pitches

from the Senators' pitcher and began to stroll leisurely toward first base.

"Why," asked Balfour, "is he not running? He's just walking."

"You see," answered Roosevelt, "he's got four balls."

"I understand," said Lord Balfour. "He would have difficulty running."

Westward Ho?

On Election Day 1916, Assistant Secretary of the Navy Roosevelt and his wife were poised for President Wilson's defeat by New York Governor Charles Evans Hughes. This time there was no three-way battle that divided the Republican vote in a nation where Republicans, since the Civil War, had dominated. The Roosevelts went to bed convinced that Wilson was defeated. They awoke to learn that, although the New York governor carried the eastern states, California and the West swung the election to Wilson.

At a press conference, FDR wryly remarked that his cousin Theodore, who supported Hughes, might be busy revising his book *The Winning of the West*.

"A Whale of a Difference"

Along with Henry Clay, another spellbinding orator, William Jennings Bryan, was the only thrice-nominated and thrice-defeated presidential candidate. Like Clay, the highest national office he would attain was secretary of state, which Bryan held under Woodrow Wilson.

In 1912 Bryan, frustrated for his fourth presidential attempt, had shifted his delegates to Wilson to break the deadlock. The number-one cabinet position was his reward.

In preparation for diplomacy, the Nebraskan Bryan, who had never been out of the country, had mastered two subjects—which did not include diplomacy and defense of the nation—God (which he was for) and gold (which he was against). In 1915, the Haitian government was threatened by an overthrow. Bryan said to Assistant Secretary of the Navy Roosevelt, "My dear fellow, send in some nearby battleships."

The urbane Roosevelt considered Bryan a bit of a bumpkin, and he would imitate the Nebraskan's prairie drawl in recalling the incident. "Mr. Secretary," said Roosevelt, "any such battleships are in Hawaii. But we do have two cruisers in Guantanamo Bay in Cuba."

"Don't get technical, Roosevelt," replied Bryan. "Send anything that has guns and floats."

"What's in a Name?"

FDR's long-time military aide was "Pa" Watson, a good ol' boy from Georgia. Once when the president was moseying in his specially altered Ford along the country roads around Warm Springs, Georgia, FDR said, "Pa, if you southerners are such believers in 'white supremacy,' how come I see so many light-skinned colored people?"

Just at that moment such a dusky specimen was seen walking down the road with a fishing pole.

Roosevelt stopped the car and asked Watson to find out the boy's father's name.

The boy replied, "I don't know."

"Do you know your own name?" pressed Watson.

"Yes, sir! It's Franklin Delano Roosevelt Jones."

"Where There's a Will, There's a Way"

At a Jefferson-Jackson Day Democratic gathering in 1935, FDR opened with a reference to one of his favorite Democratic presidents before beginning his prepared remarks.

"The Whigs were the 'economic royalist' party of another time. And those pious Whigs denounced the 'pagan' Jackson, who, up until the end of his life, never became a member of any organized faith.

"The poor Whigs were infuriated when, on his deathbed, Jackson joined a church. Said one Whig, 'Just when Jackson is about to go to hell, he cheats the devil himself and becomes a Presbyterian.'

"Well, Andy Jackson had the will to get to heaven, and he would get there; and the American people have the will to bring about a better future, and they will get there."

"A Wicked Shame"

FDR prided himself on his skills as a mixologist of cocktails. An initiation rite that accompanied being invited into the president's study was the sipping of one of the cocktails that the president poured from his shaker, such as Manhattans, old-fashioneds, and especially martinis.

Unfortunately, his concoction of three parts gin to one part vermouth assumed the sallow color of jaundice. Churchill, though not known for his religious devotion, nevertheless maintained that the blending of spirits in cocktails was blasphemous. Yet he manfully took the proffered cocktail as the president said, "Winston, I must tell you that I make a wicked martini."

Churchill, under his breath, said, "Wicked shame if you ask me."

FDR's Famous Phrases

ROOSEVELT OFTEN SPECULATED TO friends that the career he would have most enjoyed, if he had not entered politics, was advertising. He felt he had a knack for coming up with a selling line. Although Roosevelt, unlike Lincoln or Churchill, seldom wrote his own speeches, he had an innate sense of recognizing a ringing phrase when he read one or adapting one to make it catchier.

It was he who composed the rhyming and rhythmic chant mocking Republican leaders, "Martin, Barton, and Fish." As a presidential speaker, he had a natural acting talent only exceeded later by the professionally trained Ronald Reagan. Roosevelt could also spot a zinger line in a speech draft, such as "ill-fed, ill-clad, ill-housed" in his second inaugural address, or a muted rhyme like "the hand that held the dagger plunged it into the back of its neighbor."

It was FDR, not a speechwriter, who came up with the line accompanying a presidential veto, "It was not a bill for the needy but for the greedy."

Unlike many speechwriters trained in journalism, which prints for the eye, Roosevelt understood that speeches were unrhymed and unmetered verses addressed to the ear. Roosevelt, when reading the draft of a speech, had a sixth sense about a line that would be memorable. He also had mastered, like an actor, the pause before a key word or phrase. In other words, he combined a copywriter's skill for phrasing and an actor's sense of timing.

"The Happy Warrior" (1924)

The phrase is often applied to Franklin Roosevelt himself. In fact, it is a title of one of the president's many biographies. Roosevelt used the phrase to describe Governor Al Smith in a nominating speech for president at the Democratic National Convention in 1924. It certainly is more apt for the jaunty and high-humored Roosevelt, who relished campaigning, saying once, "I always love a good fight," than it was for Al Smith, who, in his late middle years, turned grumpier and more dyspeptic each year.

The phrase, however, was not originally coined by Roosevelt. It is from the poet Wordsworth: "The Happy Warrior, this is he/

Whom every man in arms would wish to be." It was not even Roosevelt's idea to use the two descriptive words, which had been suggested by Judge Joseph Proskauer, the legal adviser *cum* speechwriter for Al Smith.

Roosevelt objected to the phrase as "too precocious" for the ears of the delegates. But at Proskauer's insistence, he used it. According to Judge Proskauer's grandson, Tony Smith (the author's roommate at Williams College), Roosevelt would later take credit for the phrase, denying Proskauer any credit.

"Forgotten Man at the Bottom of the Economic Pyramid" (1932)

In April of 1932, New York Governor Franklin Roosevelt was already the leading Democratic candidate for the presidential nomination. In this Depression year, Roosevelt had assembled his "brain trust" of advisers for his campaign. In a radio address written by one of the "brain trusters," Columbia professor Raymond Moley, Roosevelt struck as a theme—the poor American suffering the most from this economic blight—"the forgotten man at the bottom of the economic pyramid."

The phrase "the forgotten man" had come from a speech of that title by, ironically, the social Darwinist William Graham Sumner of Yale in 1883.

"New Deal" (1932)

In his acceptance speech for the Democratic presidential nomination in Chicago in 1932, New York Governor Franklin Roosevelt vowed, "I pledge you, I pledge myself, to a new deal for the American people." The two words, which came to describe the Roosevelt administration and its domestic programs, were deliberately chosen. Roosevelt had idolized his cousin (and uncle by marriage) Theodore Roosevelt, who had given the name "Square Deal" to his progressive Republicanism.

Roosevelt picked up the variation, "new deal," from one of his favorite authors, Mark Twain. It appears in *A Connecticut Yankee in King Arthur's Court*.

"The Only Thing We Have to Fear Is Fear Itself" (1933)

Along with John F. Kennedy's "Ask not what your country can do for you," the most remembered line from an inaugural address was Roosevelt's "The only thing we have to fear is fear itself." It gave hope to a beleaguered nation.

Judge Samuel Rosenman, Roosevelt's principal speechwriter from his days as New York governor, supplied the line. Rosenman rhetorically improved Henry Thoreau's sentence in his *Journal* in 1852. "Nothing is so much to be feared as fear."

Fireside Chat (1933)

FDR's first executive order was "the bank holiday." It was issued a little more than a week after his inaugural address. Roosevelt wanted to spell out the need for action, as well as allay the people's fears about the closing down of banks.

He had often used the radio when he was New York's governor. Now he wanted to explain the complex factors that led to his decision. In the inaugural address, radio had been covering a historical event in the life of the nation. In this case, the White House was asking the networks to give the president radio time instead of airing their regularly scheduled programs.

Raymond Moley, who would write the president's remarks, called the various stations. He explained that the tone of the remarks would be informal and conversational. Harry C. Butcher, who wrote the script for Robert Trout, the Washington bureau chief for CBS, had Trout say, "The president wants to come into your home and sit at your fireside for a little fireside chat."

Roosevelt loved the phrase. He would deliver a "Fireside Chat" fourteen times in 1933 and altogether twenty-seven times during his presidency. Butcher, incidentally, would join the U.S. Navy in 1942. He would be the public relations officer for General Eisenhower and draft the general's Supreme Allied

Commander's radio speech that announced the invasion of Normandy on D-Day.

Good Neighbor Policy (1937)

This policy toward Latin America was announced in Roosevelt's second inaugural address. The imperative of developing better relations with our fellow republics in the New World had been pushed for four years by "brain truster" Raymond Moley. Ultimately it found an enthusiastic ear in the president, who thought the Western Hemisphere might be vulnerable to future meddling by Hitler.

The actual sentence from which the phrase emanated was "I would dedicate this nation to the policy of the good neighbor." Shortly thereafter, the president appointed young Nelson Rockefeller, who spoke Spanish, to the position of assistant secretary of state for Latin American affairs. It was Rockefeller who persuaded Mayor La Guardia of New York City to change the name of Sixth Avenue to Avenue of the Americas.

"This Generation Has a Rendezvous with Destiny" (1937)

This line from Roosevelt's second inaugural address is perhaps the most quoted of his lines—particularly in high school commencement addresses.

Thomas ("Tommy the Cork") Corcoran was not a Roosevelt speechwriter but a lawyer who drafted much of the New Deal legislation. He told the author in 1972 that if the theme of the first inaugural was about "relief," then the second was about "change" and the call to the citizenry to bring about such change.

Corcoran recited to the author the poem of the British poet Alan Seeger who died in World War I in 1916. The opening line, "I have a rendezvous with Death/At some disputed barricade" inspired the words "rendezvous with destiny," with destiny as the alliterative substitution for "death."

Corcoran made the suggestion to Roosevelt, who inserted it into Raymond Moley's draft of Roosevelt's second inaugural address.

The Garden Hose Analogy (1940)

At a press conference on December 16, 1940, the big issue reporters wanted to challenge President Roosevelt on the controversial Lend-Lease Bill that offered old U.S. destroyers to Britain in return for the United States taking over some of the British naval bases in the West Indies. Critics had called it a violation of neutrality.

To one journalist's question, the president answered, "Suppose my neighbor's home catches fire and I have a length of garden hose. Would I not lend it to him?"

Robert Sherwood, the playwright who often wrote presidential addresses, said that Roosevelt, with that answer, hit the question out of the park. It almost single-handedly won the battle in Congress for the Lend-Lease Bill. Sherwood was too modest to take credit for drafting the analogy for Roosevelt to use in the press conference.

"Arsenal of Democracy" (1940)

This phrase came to sum up the position of the United States as Britain alone battled Nazi Germany. It, of course, violated in spirit the official position of neutrality but described, in fact, America's role in shipping ammunition and matériel of war to Britain.

The sentence, "We must become the arsenal of democracy," came about in a Fireside Chat on December 27, 1940. Robert Sherwood, the playwright, in consultation with Harry Hopkins and Roosevelt, worked on the speech. Sherwood inserted this actual phrase, which originally was coined by Jean Monnet, the French exile who was assisting General Knudsen in planning future disposition and organization of supplies. Monnet is better known today as the Father of the European Community.

"The Hand That Held the Dagger" (1941)

In a 1941 commencement address to the University of Virginia in Charlottesville, President Roosevelt took note of the Hitlerian menace to democracies. France had already collapsed, and there was a dire need for American defense readiness. (The Selective Service System, or draft, would be proposed that summer.)

In an allusion to Mussolini's recent invasion of Italy, a long-time ally of the United States, Roosevelt intoned in the address, "The hand that held the dagger plunged it into the back of its neighbor. . . ."

In a discussion in 1994 with Harry Hopkins's son, Robert, at an International Churchill Society meeting in Washington, the author was told that Robert Sherwood, his father's aide, wrote the address. Sherwood, who wrote the play *Abe Lincoln of Illinois*, was inspired by Shakespeare's tragedy *Macbeth*, in which the title character, in an act of perfidy, murders his sleeping houseguest, saying, "Is this a dagger which I see before me?" Incidentally, *Macbeth* was Lincoln's favorite play, as well as that of playwright Sherwood.

Atlantic Charter (1941)

As President Roosevelt prepared for his secret meeting with Prime

Minister Churchill at Newfoundland Bay in August 1941, he had in mind a joint statement by the two leading democracies that would pronounce their common ideals and values. He was not sure what to call it—Atlantic "something"? Atlantic Statement? Atlantic Code? After all, they were meeting in the North Atlantic, the ocean that separated their two countries. It was Churchill who suggested Atlantic Charter because it had a suggestive echo of Magna Carta—that title deed of English-speaking people's rights.

The Rattlesnake Analogy (1941)

In a Fireside Chat on September 9, 1941, Roosevelt said, "When you see a rattlesnake poised to strike, you do not wait until he has struck before you crush him." The talk, developed by Robert Sherwood in consultation with Harry Hopkins and Roosevelt, was a call for rearmament that took account of the Hitler menace. The president was asking for destroyers to attack the "rattlesnake" German U-boats that were sinking U.S. Merchant Marine ships.

"United Nations" (1941)

Today these two words mean the world organization headquartered in New York City. But the phrase antedates the formation of that international institution.

Prime Minister Winston Churchill arrived in Washington, D.C., in December 1941, just after Pearl Harbor, to talk with President Roosevelt about the joint strategy of the war.

In a discussion that went late one night at the White House, Roosevelt mentioned various phrases that would describe all those nations that were opposed to those Fascist governments embracing tyranny.

Roosevelt rejected "League of Nations" as pejorative and evocative of the past defunct world organization.

According to Margaret (Daisy) Suckley, Roosevelt's cousin on his mother's side, the morning after the late-night discussion, the president awoke with the right word to replace "League of . . ."

It was "the United Nations." He wheeled into the Monroe Room, where Churchill was staying, excited to tell him. There he found the prime minister, bare and pink-fleshed, just emerging from his bath. Roosevelt immediately wheeled around and beat a retreat. It was then that Churchill said, "The king's first minister has nothing to hide from the president of the United States."

"Day of Infamy" (1941)

The actual sentence wording from which the phrase comes is the opening line of FDR's Declaration of War message to Congress on December 8, 1941.

"Yesterday, December 7th, 1941, a date which will live in infamy, the United States of America was suddenly and deliberately attacked. . . ."

It was Roosevelt himself who wrote the message, and he chose the word "infamy." The unusual word, meaning "notoriety or disgrace," is almost never heard in conversation, unless preceded by "day of. . . ." Roosevelt, who was a master of public relations, must have sensed the word would be chosen by newspapers for their headlines, which it was.

The word "infamy," which can actuate legal damages, is defined in Black's Law Dictionary. It is familiar to attorneys. FDR once assisted his cousin Theodore Roosevelt by testifying in a libel suit as to Teddy's habits of temperance. The former president claimed in his libel suit that he was a victim of "infamy" and "slander" when he had been called a "drunk." "Infamy," in that context, is the damage to reputation the libelant has caused by his words to the reputation of the libelee.

Four Freedoms (1942)

On Roosevelt's shipboard conference in Newfoundland Bay with British Prime Minister Winston Churchill, from which emanated the Atlantic Charter, Roosevelt broached the notion of "Four Freedoms"—Freedom of Speech, Freedom of Religion, Freedom from Fear—the fourth was the last to surface. Roosevelt liked the alliterative resonance of Four Freedoms. He toyed with Freedom from Hunger or Poverty. He finally settled on Freedom from Want.

On January 1, 1942, President Roosevelt, mindful that Lincoln issued his Emancipation Proclamation from the White House on New Year's Day 1863, issued the Four Freedoms proclamation. It was a democratic credo with which to fight the war with the Axis dictators—Hitler, Mussolini, and Tojo.

Unconditional Surrender (1942)

No words offered by President Roosevelt were more decisive in shaping the military course of World War II than these. The phrase was, of course, not originally coined by Roosevelt. General Ulysses S. Grant offered these two words as his implacable terms in the attack on Fort Donelson in the Civil War. The two words came to stand for the two initials before his surname—

Unconditional Surrender Grant. (His real name was Ulysses Simpson Grant.)

Yet it would become known to the world in February 1942 at a press conference in Casablanca in Morocco. After a joint communiqué by President Roosevelt and Prime Minister Churchill, in which the phrase did not appear, Roosevelt, in talking to reporters, used the phrase. According to observers, Churchill visibly winced at the phrase. Yet Churchill, following Roosevelt, felt he could not gainsay the words of his most powerful ally.

If the phrase disconcerted Prime Minister Churchill, it delighted Premier Stalin. The paranoiac Soviet dictator was relieved that the United States and Britain would not negotiate a peace with the Germans behind his back.

General Eisenhower was later to say that the terms for surrender by Germany extended the war four months from January to May. General MacArthur also opposed the "unconditional surrender" ultimatum in the war against Japan.

163

FDR's Memorable Speeches

THE SATURDAY MORNING RADIO address from the Oval Office by the nation's chief executive has become more than an embedded tradition. It is now an institution. It traces its origin back to President Franklin Roosevelt's "Fireside Chats."

Roosevelt introduced this informal radio talk to the American people. It was he who made the "Fireside Chat" a political institution. The image the president wanted to convey was that of the head of the house confiding to his family, in an intimate and candid manner, matters of mutual concern or problems that were facing the family.

Roosevelt was the first politician to master the medium of radio. He caressed the microphone in a conversational tone, not like so many politicians who almost shout their words as if they are yelling to a crowd through a megaphone, the result of which is a rant that sounds more partisan than persuasive.

Two giants of the twentieth century made the radio their personal instrument to arouse hope in their respective listeners and deliver them from fear: Franklin Roosevelt and Winston Churchill. Roosevelt, however, used the radio during the Depression some years before Churchill did as the wartime prime minister. Beginning in the 1930s, Roosevelt, as president to millions of households, made his voice the most familiar and the most recognized outside of one's immediate family. In poor white dwellings in Appalachia, as well as in black shanties in the Deep South, a portrait of Roosevelt often hung next to that of Jesus. And those families would regularly tune in to Roosevelt's frequent "Fireside Chats" as they would *Amos 'n' Andy* or *Fibber McGee & Molly*.

Churchill, who won a Nobel Prize for Literature, delivered addresses that would pass into the great works of English literature. A wit once observed that if Churchill had employed the services of a speechwriter, Britain might have been speaking German today.

In fact, in 1941, Roosevelt charged his principal aide and friend, Harry Hopkins, to find out if Churchill wrote his speeches himself. When Hopkins reported back to Roosevelt that Churchill was his own speechwriter, the president did not greet the news happily.

But Roosevelt's patrician tenor might have been a better fit for the radio than Churchill's guttural growl that featured weak consonants and strong vowels. Unlike Roosevelt, the majesty of Churchill's rhetoric lay more in his words than in his voice.

Roosevelt's radio voice inspired Ronald Reagan to first choose radio as his vocation before heading for Hollywood. Richard Nixon, who, though not telegenic, possessed a rich baritone voice. (In the Nixon-Kennedy debates of 1960, those who listened to the radio thought Nixon was clearly the winner.) Nixon also revealed that FDR's mention of his dog Fala was the inspiration for his "Checkers" talk in 1952.

Accordingly, in 1968, Nixon used short recorded radio addresses (drafted by Ray Price, a *New York Herald Tribune* editorial writer and later Nixon's number-one White House speechwriter). Then after he was elected to the presidency, it was Nixon, in imitation of Roosevelt's "Fireside Chats," who instituted the Saturday morning radio address.

No one, and that includes news commentators and crooners, ever projected such assurance and power of personality through radio as Roosevelt did.

In his early "New Deal" days, Roosevelt would recycle some of the programs his predecessor Herbert Hoover had proposed.

If Hoover failed, it was not so much because of his policies as because of his personality. Roosevelt, by his voice alone, manifested hope in such a tangible form that his listeners could almost feel it and grasp it to their bosoms.

The Presidential Nominating Speech for Governor Al Smith (1924)

The most difficult speech challenge in Roosevelt's career was his nominating address for Governor Al Smith for president at the Democratic National Convention at Madison Square Garden in New York City. That short address was important in shaping Roosevelt's political career. Without it, he probably would never have succeeded Smith as governor of New York and thus never would have advanced to the White House in the 1932 presidential election.

It was not the drafting of the talk that was the challenge but the physical ordeal of the delivery—the strenuous effort of a man with paralyzed legs to maneuver his way from his seat on the dais to the podium at the convention hall. After all, presidential nominating addresses are rarely remembered in history; they usually consist of a litany of platitudinous virtues of the proposed candidate.

Four years before, in 1920, those same Democratic delegates had nominated Franklin Roosevelt to be the vice presidential candidate with Governor James Cox of Ohio. Although it was a losing race, the assistant secretary of the navy had endeared himself to Democratic voters during his railroad campaign across America. Like his cousin, Theodore Roosevelt in 1900 when he was running with President McKinley, Franklin Roosevelt was the face and spokesman of the campaign, while the two presidential nominees had conducted their respective campaigns from their front porches.

But less than a half year after that election, Franklin Roosevelt was stricken with polio. Rumors were rife that he was a helpless cripple—and cripples had no future in politics.

Governor Al Smith at first balked when it was suggested to him by his top aide and adviser, Judge Joseph Proskauer, that Roosevelt deliver the nominating address. Smith, a professional politician who had risen through Tammany Hall, considered the former New York Democratic state senator Roosevelt a dilettante and lightweight.

The original choice was the Irish-American statesman Bourke Cockran, considered by William Howard Taft to be "America's greatest orator." Thrice Cockran had been the keynote speaker for the Democratic National Convention. Cockran was also the rhetorical mentor of Winston Churchill, who deemed Cockran the most gifted speaker he had ever heard.

In the play *Sunrise at Campobello*, a dying Cockran is heard to say, "Frank, get off your sick bed and give the speech. I won't be able to."

Actually, Proskauer's reasons for replacing Cockran with Roosevelt were purely political. He told Al Smith, "Al, you are a Mick from the Bowery—Roosevelt is a Yankee Protestant from up-state." Smith reluctantly agreed, and Roosevelt was approached. Roosevelt said "yes" on the condition that Proskauer write the speech. Proskauer was a former New York judge who was Governor Smith's legal counsel. (Proskauer in ethnic background and duties was to Smith what Judge Sam Rosenman would be later for the governor and then President Roosevelt.)

Roosevelt rejected Judge Proskauer's draft, particularly the "Happy Warrior" reference as too "precious," and Roosevelt wrote his own speech. Proskauer found Roosevelt's draft trite and superficial and insisted that he go with the original speech. An adamant Roosevelt suggested that they take it to an impartial critic, Herbert Bayard Swope, the respected editor of the *New York World*. Much to Roosevelt's chagrin, Swope sided with Proskauer. Roosevelt agreed to read Proskauer's version, but he warned that it would be a flop.

But Roosevelt was more worried about the logistics than the

rhetoric. He wanted to dispel any image of a "cripple" in his procession to the platform. A wheelchair was out of the question. Accordingly, Roosevelt arrived an hour earlier than he had to, with his sons James and Elliott to lean on as he walked while the hall was half empty. Some young, cheering women with long, trailing dresses closely followed Roosevelt, hiding the view of his crutches while he maneuvered his leg braces with his sons supporting him to make his way slowly up the aisle.

As Roosevelt climbed to the platform, the delegates could not see the braces and the awkward ascent of Roosevelt to the seats behind the presiding chairman.

When Roosevelt was introduced, he made his way to the podium, still holding on to his sons for support. At the last moment, he swung himself forward by his crutches and grabbed the edge of the speaker's stand. Exhausted and panting from the effort, he was able to collect himself as the audience roared to their feet applauding the man whom they had nominated for vice president four years before.

With his rich and melodious voice and Harvard accent, he made the cadence of words both intimate and informal. Roosevelt kept to the Proskauer draft, except for a quotation from Lincoln, which Roosevelt had inserted in his own version:

*You equally who come from the great cities of the East
and from the plains and the hills of the West and from
the homes and fields of the Southland, I ask you, in all
sincerity, in balloting on that platform tomorrow, to keep
first in your hearts and minds the words of Abraham Lincoln, "With malice toward none; with charity toward all."*

Roosevelt's use of the quotation was meant to reach out to the
anti-Catholic Protestant delegates, and it stirred applause.

In his closing paragraph, Roosevelt delivered those Proskauer
phrasings that came to forever mark the nominating speech as
the "Happy Warrior" talk:

*He has the power to strike at error and wrongdoing that
makes his adversaries quail before him. He has a personality that carries to every bearer not only the sincerity
but the righteousness of what he says. He is the "Happy
Warrior" of the political battlefield.*

Though the bells signaled a wild demonstration for Governor
Smith, it was Roosevelt who proved to be the most popular figure at the convention. Roosevelt had reestablished himself as a

Democratic national leader who could appeal to all factions and sections of the country.

The 1932 Convention Acceptance Speech

Roosevelt chose to fly a plane to Chicago. Just as he was the first governor to regularly use another twentieth-century invention—the radio, Roosevelt saw the plane as a symbol of this new age of technology. Roosevelt was signaling that he would be a leader, abreast of the new developments of this new era. It would be a contrast to President Hoover, whose stiff collars seemed emblematic of old ideas as well as old fashions.

Roosevelt's longtime aide, Louis Howe, met him at the airport in Chicago. Howe, who had orchestrated the moves leading to Roosevelt's nomination for president at the convention, handed the governor the draft he had prepared for Roosevelt's acceptance speech.

Unbeknownst to Howe, Roosevelt already had a draft with him, which had been prepared by Raymond Moley, his "brain truster" from Columbia University.

Addressing the delegates in what Al Smith would call "his cultured and modulated voice," Roosevelt opened with the first lines of Howe's address. It confused Moley, who was following with the agreed-upon speech that he had drafted. But Roosevelt, as a gesture to his old aide since his state senate days, wanted to make Howe a coauthor of this address, which would be the culmination of Howe's lifework. So Roosevelt began by alluding to his plane trip, in Howe's words, "My appearance today is unprecedented and unusual." (If the second adjective was made redundant by the first, it had the rhetorical flourish of two words beginning with "un.")

Then Governor Roosevelt shifted to the Moley draft:

Ours must be a party of liberal thought, of planned action, of enlightened international outlook of the greatest good to the greatest number of citizens.

Roosevelt outlined a preview of his presidential programs: job creation through emergency public works, the end of Prohibition, mortgage relief, and lower tariffs.

Roosevelt then enunciated his political philosophy:

Never before in modern history have the essential differences between the two major parties stood out in such striking contrast as they do today. Republican leaders not only have failed in material things, they have failed in national vision because in disaster they have held out no hope, they have pointed out no path for the people below to climb back both to places of security and of safety in our American life.

He delivered his closing peroration:

I pledge you, I pledge myself to a new deal for the American people. Let us all here assembled constitute ourselves prophets of a new order of competence and of courage. This is more than a political campaign; it is a call to arms. Give me your help, not to win votes alone, but to win in this crusade to restore America to its own people.

The words "new deal" might not have become the catchword of the Roosevelt administration but for Herbert Bayard Swope, the editor of the *New York World*. He had written an article a couple of days after FDR's acceptance speech, which alluded to FDR's cousin Teddy's use of "Square Deal," as well as a reference to Mark Twain's coinage of the phrase.

The First Inaugural Address (1933)

On Inauguration Day, March 4, 1933, crowds massed in front of the Capitol, despite icy winds. That winter, the Depression had more deeply pierced the heart of America. In the midst of mounting unemployment, agitators calling for revolution toppled over milk trucks and stormed banks, while the financial structure of the nation teetered on collapse.

Six days before the inauguration, Governor Roosevelt was in his Hyde Park study reviewing the draft of his speech, which had been prepared by Raymond Moley, one of the "brain trusters" whom he had recruited from Columbia University. The speech had been edited and shortened by Roosevelt's top adviser, Judge Samuel Rosenman. On a lined legal-sized yellow pad, Roosevelt had made notes and additions.

As he waited in the U.S. Senate chambers before proceeding to the inaugural stand, Roosevelt penned an opening line to the finished typed text. "This is a day of consecration."

But as he stood at the stand after the cheers died, he ad-libbed to emend that opening in a ringing voice, "This is a day of national consecration." As millions huddled around their radios, Roosevelt issued his triumphant call:

*First of all, let me assert my firm belief that the only thing
we have to fear is fear itself.*

In a rhetorical device used by Athenian orators like Pericles,
Roosevelt had preceded that line with a prefatory line to ensure
attention and later quotability for this ringing phrase that echoed
the word *fear*. Roosevelt then flung back his head and intoned:

*In every dark hour of our national life, a leadership of
frankness and vigor has met with that understanding and
support of the people themselves, which is essential to victory. I am convinced that you again will give that support
to leadership in these critical days.*

Then followed an adagio provided by Moley in softer terms:

*Values have shrunken to fantastic levels; taxes have risen; our
ability to pay has fallen. Government of all kinds is faced by
serious curtailment of income; the means of exchange are fro-
zen in the currents of trade; the withered leaves of industrial
enterprise lie on every side; farmers find no markets for their
produce; the savings of many years in thousands of families*

are gone. More important, a host of unemployed citizens face the grim problem of existence and an equally great number toil with little return. Only a foolish optimist can deny the dark realities of the moment.

In two biblical allusions from first the Old Testament (Proverbs) and then the New Testament (Gospel of Matthew), Roosevelt then denounced Wall Street and big business in lines that he himself added:

They have no vision, and when there is no vision, the people perish. The money changers have fled from their high seats in the temple of civilization.

The partisan crowd at first was restrained but then burst into applause as Roosevelt continued:

This nation asks for action and action now. . . . We must act and act quickly. We must move as a trained and loyal army, willing to sacrifice for the good of a common discipline, because without such discipline, no progress is made, no leadership effective.

In an untypically grim tone for Roosevelt, he directed a challenge to Congress:

I shall ask the Congress for the one remaining instrument to meet the crisis—broad Executive power to wage a war against an emergency, as great as the power that would be given to me if we were invaded by a foreign foe.

The crowd then thundered into its longest applause of the day. Roosevelt's wife later remarked that it scared her to hear how close the country had come to accepting a dictatorship.

The unsmiling president then closed with a firm warning:

We do not distrust the future of essential democracy. The people of the United States have not failed. In their need, they have registered a mandate that they want direct vigorous action. They have made me the present instrument of these wishes. In the spirit of the gift, I take it.

FDR's First Fireside Chat
March 12, 1933

The first executive action the newly sworn-in president took was closing down the banks. Roosevelt decided to address the nation on radio for two reasons: first, to allay the fears of the American people of this unprecedented presidential action, and second, to reinforce the impression that he would be a decisive president ready to take any steps to meet the economic challenges facing the nation.

Roosevelt had been the first governor to use the radio extensively. Now he would be the first president. Of course, radio had covered previous presidents in their inaugural addresses. But Roosevelt would make the radio his personal instrument. The White House had called the networks and orchestrated with them the timing of the talk. The date of the bank closing was coordinated with FDR's scheduled talk. The term "Fireside Chat" was suggested to Roosevelt, and he readily adopted it to describe his talk. It was to suggest both intimacy and informality—which would be the future ingredients of Roosevelt's radio talks with the American people and the establishment of a personal bond with them.

The speech was drafted by "brain truster" Raymond Moley, with additions and the closing by Judge Sam Rosenman.

Note how the president begins:

My friends, I want to talk for a few minutes with the people of the United States about banking.

The president then explains the danger when too many worried depositors withdraw money and banks are pressed to meet the demand for currency. This was the president's reason for a "bank holiday":

We had a bad banking situation. Some of our bankers had shown themselves either incompetent or dishonest in their handling of the situation. . . .

I do not promise you that every bank will be reopened or that individual losses will not be suffered, but there will be no losses that possibly could be avoided, and there would have been more and greater losses had we continued to draft.

FDR then closed his talk with his inaugural theme of faith against fear:

After all there is an element in the readjustment of our financial structure more important than currency, more important than gold. That is the confidence of the people. Confidence and courage are the essentials of success in carrying out the plan. You people must have faith; you must not be stampeded by rumors or guesses. Let us unite in banishing fear. We have provided the machinery to restore our financial system; it is up to you to support and make it work.

It is your problem, no less than mine. Together we cannot fail.

I Hate War

Lake Chautauqua, New York, August 1936

In the summer of 1936, the menacing figure of Adolf Hitler was casting his shadow of war across Europe. A rearmed Germany had marched its troops into the Rhineland in violation of the Versailles Treaty. The Nazi Führer had signed an Axis pact with the Fascist Il Duce, Benito Mussolini of Italy. Both countries were supporting the Fascist Generalissimo Franco of the Nationalists in Spain during the Civil War against the Republicans.

In the wake of these developments, the Chautauqua Association, one of the oldest and most prestigious lecture forums in the world, invited President Roosevelt to deliver an address. Lake Chautauqua is located in the southwest corner of New York state. In the nineteenth century, the Methodists had established a summer colony there, with an open-air auditorium for lectures on spiritual, political, and literary subjects. That association had spawned women's clubs in major cities in the United States, which would invite lecturers of national opinion to speak.

As a boy, FDR and his mother had visited the lake community and had heard several lectures. In the 1930s some of the speakers included such noted figures as world traveler Lowell Thomas, author John Gunther, and novelists Sinclair Lewis and Pearl S. Buck. The Chautauqua Association prided itself on hosting the most eloquent orators in the country.

In this reelection year, Roosevelt would rise to the oratorical challenge and deliver a lyrical masterpiece on the atrocity of war.

In his campaign for vice president in 1920, in supporting the League of Nations, Roosevelt had alluded to his experiences as assistant secretary of the navy, when he visited the war front in France. In the ensuing years, Roosevelt's memories of his brief visit to the battlefield while attending a Paris conference grew more embellished in the repeated retelling.

Judge Sam Rosenman wrote the initial draft, but the president himself rewrote it. His sentences toward the end of the address, with their repetitive verb forms and eye-provoking descriptions of war's havoc and horror in the following paragraph, are Churchillian.

I have seen war. I have seen war on land and sea. I have seen blood running from the wounded. I have seen men coughing out their gassed lungs. I have seen the dead in the mud. I have seen cities destroyed. I have seen two hundred limping, exhausted men come out of line — the survivors of a regiment of one thousand that went forward forty-eight hours before. I have seen children starving. I have seen the agony of mothers and wives. I hate war.

Less poetically, Roosevelt concluded:

I have passed unnumbered hours, I shall pass unnumbered hours thinking and planning how war may be kept from this nation.

I wish I could keep war from all nations, but that is beyond my power. I can at least make certain that no act of the United States helps to produce or to promote war. I can

at least make clear that the conscience of America revolts
against war and that any nation which provokes war for-
feits the sympathy of the people of the United States. . . .

The Second Inaugural Address (1937)

For the first time in history, a president delivered his inaugural address in January, not in March. The Twentieth Amendment, ratified a few years before, effected that change. Roosevelt in his speech wanted to dramatize the differences that had taken place from the previous four years. Unlike 1933, the skies that January were sunny, not cloudy. Roosevelt, with his confident voice, opened by assuring everyone that happier days lay in the future:

When four years ago we met to inaugurate a president,
the Republic, single-minded in adversity, stood in spirit
here. We dedicated ourselves to a vision that would speed
the time when there would be for all the people the secu-
rity and peace essential to the pursuit of happiness.

Roosevelt then reiterated the biblical reference in his first inaugural:

We of the Republic pledged ourselves to drive from the

*temple of our ancient faith those who profaned it; to end
by action—tireless and unafraid—the stagnation and
despair of the day.*

Toward the end of the address, the president added:

*Have we reached the goal of our vision on the fourth day
of March 1933? Have we found our happy valley? . . .*

But here is the challenge to our democracy. . . .

*I see millions denied education, recreation, and the oppor-
tunity to better their lot and the lot of their children.*

*I see millions lacking the means to buy the products of
farm and factory and by their poverty denying work and
productiveness to many other millions.*

Roosevelt then paused as he delivered the most quoted and
memorable line of the address:

*I see one-third of a nation ill-housed, ill-clad, and ill-
nourished.*

Roosevelt's resonant voice did justice to the crafted line of

Sam Rosenman, and the words gave hope to millions who listened to their radio in their shanties and hovels.

The Second Bill of Rights Address (1941)

In his State of the Union Address to Congress in January 1941, Roosevelt would deliver what his liberal Democrats would later seize on as the foundation for a postwar agenda. Roosevelt, in his address, was advancing an issue to frame for the midterm election of 1942.

Roosevelt reasserted again the freedoms that he had earlier called for—freedom of speech and freedom of religion—but added two more: freedom from fear and freedom from want:

> *Essential to peace is a decent standard of living for all individual men and women and children in all nations. Freedom from fear is eternally linked with freedom from want. . . .*

FDR then specified what he called

> *. . . a second Bill of Rights under which a new basis for security and prosperity can be established for all—regardless of station, race, or creed.*

Included was a right to

*. . . a useful and remunerative job; the right to earn
enough to provide adequate food and clothing and recreation; the right of every businessman, large and small,
to trade in an atmosphere of freedom from unfair competition and from domination by monopolies at home or
abroad.*

And he then added:

*. . . the right of every family to a decent home; the right to
adequate medical care; the right to adequate protection
from the economic fears of old age, sickness, accident,
and unemployment; and the right to a good education.*

The Declaration of War (1941)

At 10:30 A.M., December 7, 1941, President Roosevelt received
the final Japanese reply to U.S. proposals for peace. Just after
lunch, at 1:40 P.M., the president heard the first reports that Pearl
Harbor was under bombardment. At about three o'clock, the
president telephoned Prime Minister Churchill, who was dining

at Chequers (the prime minister's country residence) with U.S. Ambassador John Winant and Roosevelt's special envoy, Averell Harriman. Said the president to Churchill, "We're all in the same boat now."

After telephoning congressional leaders, the president called for a special session of Congress the next day, Monday, at 12:30 P.M. Roosevelt then proceeded to write a brief message to accompany his declaration of war.

As he was drafting his speech, the president could hear large crowds singing patriotic songs outside the White House fence, such as "God Bless America" and "America, the Beautiful."

Without any medication, he went to sleep soundly at 10:30 P.M. The next morning, after breakfast, he added to the draft he had written the reports of the latest Japanese attacks and landings.

The president's brief but eloquent speech to Congress was broadcast throughout the world. It has to be one of the most famous and successful speeches of his career. Powerfully delivered in his measured and resolute voice, he caught the mood of the American people and Congress.

Yesterday, December 7, 1941—a date which will live

*in infamy—the United States of America was suddenly
and deliberately attacked by naval and air forces of the
Empire of Japan.*

*The United States was at peace with that nation and at
the solicitation of Japan was still in conversation with its
government and its emperor.*

After emphasizing the perfidy and treachery of the Japanese,
Roosevelt recited a litany of their attacks and the loss of American lives. He then added:

*No matter how long it may take us to overcome this
premeditated invasion, the American people, in their righ-
teous might, will win through to absolute victory.*

Roosevelt then closed by stating:

*. . . with confidence in our armed forces, with the un-
bounding determination of our people, we will gain the
inevitable triumph, so help us God.*

The use of *unbounding* (instead of the more proper *unbounded*) and *infamy* is proof that Roosevelt himself, and not one of his writers, wrote the speech. *Unbounding* is a sailor's adjective, and *infamy* is a lawyer's word. Roosevelt used words not ever heard before in presidential speeches or in any other American statesman's speeches.

The Fala Speech (1944)

In September 1944, President Roosevelt's chances for winning a fourth term were slipping. Polls were showing that Governor Dewey, the Republican candidate, was pulling up close to Roosevelt. Even the wartime adage of Abraham Lincoln was questioned. ("Don't change horses in the middle of the stream.") Roosevelt, to continue the analogy, looked like a tired, weary, and even a feeble horse.

Roosevelt had to show his Democratic legions and the American people that he was still in campaign fettle. Although Dewey never directly named the health issue, the Republican candidate had called for a "new" and "vigorous" leadership, fanning the underground rumors, by implication, that the president would never complete another term.

The speech to the Teamsters Union at the Statler Hotel in

Washington, D.C., on September 23, 1944, was the occasion for Roosevelt to scotch the health rumors.

He began from his place at the podium:

Well, here we are together again—after four years—what years they have been! You know I am actually four years older [and here he rolled his eyes upward], *which is a fact that seems to annoy some people. In fact, there are millions of people who are more than eleven years older than when we started to clean up the mess that was dumped in our laps in 1933.*

Then he would allude to some of the progressive-sounding statements of Dewey:

Now imitation may be the sincerest form of flattery, but in this case, it is the most obvious common or garden variety of fraud.

Roosevelt continued:

If it is true that there are enlightened liberal elements in

*the Republican Party . . . But can this Old Guard pass
itself off as the New Deal? We have all seen many marvel-
ous stunts in the circus, but no performing elephant could
turn a handspring without falling on its back.*

The crowd now erupted in uproarious applause.

Then in the best political humor ever seen in a presidential
campaign, Roosevelt responded to Republican attacks that he
had sent a destroyer to Alaska to retrieve his Scottish terrier,
Fala:

*These Republican leaders have not been content with at-
tacks on me, my wife, or my sons.*

[This he added in mock sorrowful tones.]

*No, not content with that, they now include my little dog,
Fala.*

The audience began to roar.

Well, of course, I don't resent the attacks, and my family doesn't resent the attacks, but Fala does resent them.

Then with both brows arched high on his forehead:

You know Fala is Scotch and being a Scottie, as soon as
he learned that the Republican fiction writers in Con-
gress had concocted a story that I left him behind on the
Aleutian Islands and had sent a destroyer back to find
him—at a cost of two or three or eight or twenty million
dollars—his Scotch soul was furious. He has not been the
same dog since.

The volume of laughter in the ballroom hit a high-water
mark. Roosevelt waited for the laughter to subside and added:

I am accustomed to hearing malicious falsehoods
about myself, such as that old worm-eaten chestnut
that I have represented myself as indispensable. But
I think I have a right to object to libelous statements
about my dog.

The speech was a resurrection of the old fighting Roosevelt. Harry Hopkins, FDR's top aide, thought it was the best campaign speech ever made. And Judge Rosenman, who had been writing speeches for Roosevelt for seventeen years, also acclaimed it as the best speech FDR ever made.

The Fourth Inaugural Address (1945)

On New Year's Day, 1945, President Roosevelt had other things more important on his mind than the upcoming inauguration festivities in a few weeks. The dominant concern was his scheduled trip to Yalta in February to meet Prime Minister Winston Churchill and Premier Joseph Stalin at the Big Three conference.

Because he wanted to conserve his weakening frame for the arduous trip, FDR decided to move the ceremonies from the Capitol to the White House, which, in effect, ruled out his having to sit in a box to observe a long parade on a winter afternoon.

Roosevelt was trying implicitly to manifest the message that wartime was no occasion for frivolity. So he would deliver a short speech—the briefest inaugural address ever—that would reinforce the idea that he, like the soldiers, sailors, and civilians, had to get back to work.

There was another benefit of a short speech. The effort of standing in steel braces for a lengthy time would have been too much of an ordeal. He would have to save his dwindling reserves for his trek across the globe next month to Yalta.

The president had tinkered with a draft written by Robert Sherwood, but in the end, his speech reflected FDR's own personal thoughts.

Before almost five thousand people in a snow-packed Washington, Roosevelt was sworn in on the family Bible, which dated back to 1686. It was open to First Corinthian's thirteenth chapter. "And now abideth faith, hope, and charity, but the greatest of these is charity." Chief Justice Harlan Stone, who had replaced Charles Evans Hughes, did the swearing in while Roosevelt's son, James, held his arm. Then Roosevelt gave his address:

Mr. Chief Justice, Mr. Vice President, and friends. You will understand that the form of this inauguration will be simple and its words brief. We Americans of today, together with our allies, are passing thorough a supreme test. It is a test of our courage—of our resolve—of our wisdom—and of our essential democracy. . . .

We have learned that we cannot live alone, at peace; that our well-being is dependent on the well-being of other nations far away. . . .

We have learned to be citizens of the world, members of the human community. . . .

So we pray to Him now for a vision to see our way clearly —to see the way that leads to a better life for ourselves, and for our fellow men—and to the achievement of His will to peace on earth.

Although it was only a six-minute talk, Roosevelt felt the strain. He told his son, Jimmy, that he had a pain in his heart. "Give me a stiff drink. You better make it a straight one."

His Last Words (1945)

In April of 1945, a frail and spent President Roosevelt needed a chance to rest and recoup his dwindling energies. The winter Big Three meeting with Churchill and Stalin at the Yalta Conference had left him near total exhaustion.

Accordingly, the president journeyed by train to Warm Springs, Georgia, whose hot mineral waters, for two decades, had been a tonic not only for his body but for his spirits as well.

At the arrangement of his daughter, Anna, his longtime intimate friend Lucy Mercer Rutherford joined him. She was the former social secretary to Roosevelt when he was assistant secretary of the navy during World War I. Their romance had almost broken up the Roosevelt marriage. Now a widow, she had secretly met several times with the president on railway stops in New Jersey near where she lived.

The president had one item on his agenda during his Warm Springs sojourn—preparation for the Jefferson-Jackson Day address, which would be read by him on the telephone on April 13. He knew that the German surrender had to be only weeks, maybe a month, away. The theme had to be the planning for postwar peace.

The Democratic National Committee had prepared a draft, which Roosevelt disliked because of its turgid and mechanical litany of proposed domestic legislation. Roosevelt had sent the draft to Robert Sherwood, the playwright who worked with Harry Hopkins.

While at Warm Springs, Roosevelt was also posing for a portrait by Elizabeth Shoumatoff, who had painted a portrait the year before in which his shoulders had been covered by a navy-blue cape.

Roosevelt's daughter, Anna, had particularly liked the portrait, and the artist had traveled with Lucy Mercer Rutherford from the Rutherfords' winter home in Aiken, South Carolina, to Warm Springs.

As FDR sat for the portrait on April 12, he added an ending to the draft on a yellow-lined legal sheet.

Today, as we move against the terrible scourge of war—as we go forward towards the greatest contribution that any generation of human beings can make in this world—the contribution of lasting peace, I ask you to keep up your faith. I measure the sound, solid achievement that can be made at this time by the straight edge of your own confidence and your resolve.

And then what would be his last written words—the message of a dying president to his countrymen.

JAMES C. HUMES

And to you, and to all Americans who dedicate themselves with us to the making of an abiding peace, I say, the only limit to our realization of tomorrow will be our doubts of today. Let us move forward with strong and active faith.

Those were the words found by his hand as he slumped over with a cerebral stroke.

Milestones

1882   Born in Hyde Park, New York

1900   Graduated Groton School

1904   Graduated Harvard

1910   Elected to the New York State Senate

1913   Appointed assistant secretary of the navy serving President Woodrow Wilson

1920   Defeated as Democratic vice presidential candidate running with James M. Cox

1921   Afflicted with poliomyelitis at Campobello Island, New Brunswick, Canada

1924   Delivers nominating speech for Governor Alfred Smith at the Democratic National Convention held at Madison Square Garden

1928	Elected governor of New York
1930	Reelected governor of New Yprk
1932	Elected president of the United States, defeating President Herbert Hoover
1936	Reelected president, defeating Governor Alfred Landon
1938	Defeated in Supreme Court Reorganization Bill
1940	Reelected for unprecedented third term, defeating Wendell Willkie
1941	December 8, declares war against Japan and Germany after the bombing of Pearl Harbor
1944	Commander in chief for the June D-Day invasion at Normandy
1944	Reelected for fourth term, defeating Governor Thomas E. Dewey
1945	Died at Warm Springs, Georgia

Bibliography

The Autobiography of Eleanor Roosevelt

Closest Companion [Diary of Margaret "Daisy" Suckley],
    edited by Geoffrey C. Ward

*The Defining Moment: FDR's Hundred Days and the
    Triumph of Hope* by Jonathan Alter

Eleanor Roosevelt (Volumes 1-3) by Blanche Wiesen Cook

FDR: A Biography by Ted Morgan

FDR: An Intimate History by Nathan Miller

FDR: The Beckoning of Destiny by Kenneth S. Davis

FDR's Last Year by Jim Bishop

Franklin D. Roosevelt by Patrick Renshaw

Franklin D. Roosevelt: The Apprenticeship by Frank Freidel

Franklin D. Roosevelt: Launching the New Deal
    by Frank Freidel

Franklin D. Roosevelt: The Ordeal by Frank Freidel

Franklin D. Roosevelt: The Triumph by Frank Freidel

Franklin Delano Roosevelt by Roy Jenkins

Franklin Roosevelt: Champion of Freedom by Conrad Black

Memorable Quotations of Franklin D. Roosevelt, compiled
    by E. Taylor Parks and Lois F. Parks

No Ordinary Time by Doris Kearns Goodwin

Presidential Anecdotes by Paul Boller

Quotations from Franklin Delano Roosevelt, edited by the
    Republican National Committee

Roosevelt and Hopkins by Robert Sherwood

The Roosevelt Myth by John T. Flynn

Roosevelt: The Lion and the Fox by James MacGregor Burns

Roosevelt: The Soldier of Freedom by
    James MacGregor Burns

A Time for War by Robert Smith Thompson

An Untold Story: The Roosevelts of Hyde Park
    by Elliott Roosevelt and James Brough

The Wisdom and Wit of Franklin D. Roosevelt, edited
    by Peter and Helen Beilenson